History of Taunton Bay: Mining, Shipping, & Diving

Franklin, Hancock, & Sullivan, Maine

John and Marlene Daley

The Galley Publishing

Published by The Galley Publishing
U.S. Highway 1
1715 Sullivan, Maine 04664
tauntonbay@hotmail.com

Front Cover Design by Jessie, Tashia and Jennie Daley,
*Sullivan Sorrento Historical Society, Denver Library, Daley
Collection*
Back Cover Design by Jessie, Tashia Jennie Daley, *Daley
Collection, Sullivan Sorrento Historical Society, Denver
Library, Jackie Weaver*

Editor
Michael Heyden

First Published 2017

Manufactured in the United States
ISBN 978.0.9990972.0.5

Library of Congress Cataloging-in-Publication Data
John and Marlene Daley

History of Taunton Bay: Mining, Shipping, Diving
(Franklin, Hancock, Sullivan, Maine)

We would like to dedicate the writing of this book to our three beautiful, bright, daughters, Jessie, Tashia, and Jennie. We cannot express how proud we are of all three of them and on how much joy they bring to us. They have been and will always be the most important people in our lives. We would, also, like to dedicate the writing of this book to our parents: John's parents Martha (Daley) Stroup and his step-father Philip Stroup; and the late Gerald Daley and Marlene's parents late Arnold and Dossie Tash Sr. They have instilled in us the importance of education and history. We have always treasured the time we have spent with our families.

Contents

Acknowledgements...........................5
Introduction.................................7

Part I   Of the Land and the Sea
  1.   Sullivan Falls and Sullivan Harbor..9
  2.   Taunton Bay Crossings..............59

Part II   Of the Sea, the Men and the
Mishaps
  3.   Crabtree Ledge Lighthouse.........79
  4.   Schooner Mabel E. Goss..........104
  5.   Schooner Abbie Bursley..........131
  6.   Schooner William Gillum.........153

Part III Of Mines and Men
  7.   Mining the Sullivan Lode.........167
  8.   Pine Tree Silver Mining Co. 192
  9.   Faneuil Hall Mining Company....210
  10.   Sullivan Mining Company.........225
  11.   Milton Mining and Milling Co. ..245

Epilogue....................................293
Bibliography................................294
About the Authors...........................304

ACKNOWLEDGEMENTS

We would like to thank the Sullivan Sorrento Historical Society and assistance from Barbara Potter, and Gary and Jeanne Edwards. Mrs. Potter, and Mr. and Mrs. Edwards were of great importance in helping us gather some of the local photographs. We would like thank the Maritime Archaeological Historical Society for the knowledge gained from their educational program. A special thanks to the Maine Historical Preservation Commission and Director Kirk F. Mohney for providing us with photographs.

We would like to thank all the divers who contributed countless hours into helping us advance our knowledge in the history of Taunton Bay. Some of the divers were, Royce Gordon, Kenneth Grant DM, Paul Savoy DM, Dean Smith DM, Jason Jamison DM, Brad Kennedy, Jeff Leighton, Mark Andrews DM, Jessie Daley, John Murphy, Megan McGonagle, Frank Salonick, Jennie Daley, Tyler Norton, Aaron Herzog, Aaron Gilpatrick DM, Eric Doak, Mike Look, Nick Simmons, and Zack Simmons. Harry Fish DM who was indispensable in helping us identify ship artifacts. Harry volunteered countless hours and the use of his own boat. We are most grateful for the hours the University of Maine at Machias dive students put into helping us within the research and exploration.

We owe gratitude to Howard and Helen Gordon, for the countless stories they have told us about the local area.

Thanks goes out to the Bangor Public Library, Bangor, Maine and for their collection of the *Maine Mining Journal*; Ellsworth Public Library and Hancock County Court of Deeds, Ellsworth, Maine; and Merrill Library, UMM, and Porter Memorial Library, Machias, Maine, were of unmeasurable importance in validating our research information.

Many people assisted us in this project and it would be best described as a collaborative effort by our family members and for those who have passed. John's father, Gerald Daley, and his grandmother, Jessie Daley, told many stories which helped us develop theories for this book.

The greatest support for this book goes to our daughters, Jessie, Tashia, and Jennie; and John's mother and stepfather, Martha and Philip Stroup. They have helped us with our businesses and have been a constant supporter of our endeavors.

Introduction

Taunton Bay is located at the head of Frenchman's Bay in Hancock County, Maine. The Bay is approximately

Courtesy Jennie Daley

eight miles north from the town of Bar Harbor. It has long been known for having extreme currents recorded up to thirteen knots. Taunton Bay also contains Sullivan Falls which is the largest reversing falls in North America. The wildlife and marine life are diverse and have developed a unique ecosystem within the bay. Taunton Bay is the furthest northern range for the breeding of the horseshoe crab. Its past and present marine economy is that of fishing for scallops, lobsters, crabs, clams, blood worms, sand worms, kelp, oysters,

7

urchins, mussels and salmon farming. The businesses that were developed around the bay were as risky as the currents. There was shipbuilding, commercial wharfs, quarrying, and silver, copper, and gold mines along the shores of the bay. It would be hard to believe that any area in Maine with the same relatively small geographic landscape would have such a rich history. The people and their businesses are explored in a historical manner and present day investigation. The authors, John and Marlene Daley recorded the bay's history through interviews, research, photographs, and personal investigation. Our exploration and investigation into the mines and shipwrecks of the bay makes this book unique which goes along with a truly uniqueness of Taunton Bay.

Sullivan Falls and Sullivan Harbor

Sullivan Falls, also referred to as Tidal Falls, is the inlet and outlet for three upper bays; Taunton, Hog, and Egypt; and the lower bay called Frenchman's Bay. The falls is about one-fourth the width of Taunton Bay, the lower of the three bays. Taunton is about one-half the width of the two upper bays. On the Sullivan side of the Sullivan Falls, the shore goes up a steep rocky embankment. On the Hancock side, the shore is made up of flat ledges with a gradual slope to the tree line. In the center of the Sullivan Falls, there is an island referred to as the center ledge. This center ledge has been the area of numerous wrecks. The length of the falls is approximately 1000 feet. The water gorges in and out during the exchange of the tides; leading to its name Tidal Falls. Whirlpools and eddies are plentiful in this waterway. The current through Tidal Falls can reach a speed of thirteen knots.

The area was inhabited by a mysterious race long before Europeans cast their eyes upon Tidal Falls. The earliest race to make a home in the Sullivan Falls area was referred to as "The Red Paint People." They were known to be in the area up to 7,000 years ago; long before the Algonquian Indians were in the area. It is debated in some academic circles as to whether the Red Paint People were a separate race different from North American Indian Tribes. Very little is known about who they were and where they came from originally. There is only speculation about what may have caused their total demise. Today, there are only fourteen identified Red Paint People's cemeteries in Maine. They were not a wandering group but most likely stayed in one or two locations during the year. It is believed that they stayed in areas along the coast or on waterways. What is known is that they were seafaring people. Their diet was of game, seafood, shellfish, and they even ate swordfish. They started fires by striking hard stones together to create a spark. The tools they made were most suitably used for carving and cutting wood. Their tools were made out of stone since they did not know how to smelt metals. Upon their death, their handmade stone tools were placed beside them in their graves because they believed in an afterlife. They had organized graveyards and dug their graves 30 to 40 inches deep but no deeper than 52 inches. They covered the top layers of the graves with ochre. Red ochre is formed from red hematite and iron oxide. They made a red paint concoction from the ochre with possibly fish oil or seal oil. From this practice, their name originated, The Red Paint People.

On the Hancock side of Sullivan Falls in 1885, railroad tracks were being laid for the Mt. Desert Ferry Terminal. A work crew uncovered a graveyard of Red Paint People. The graveyard is located near the Taunton Bay shoreline off from the old rail bed and is about 70 feet above sea level. During the construction, twenty graves were disturbed. The graves were found to be in two rows with a 15 foot separation between the rows. The work crew discovered two ash pits within the vicinity of the graveyard. Near the cemetery, there are two shell heaps. The soil is mostly sandy gravel with a gentle slope. Red ochre covered all of the graves. During the railroad construction, workers removed many finely crafted stone tools. They gave the artifacts to a local blacksmith who displayed them in a tub for the curious onlookers. Some of the tools were saved and sent to the Peabody Museum at Harvard University.

On July 3, 1913, Warren K. Moorehead was head of The Philips Academy Archaeology Department in Andover, Massachusetts. He led an archeological dig near Sullivan Falls. They stayed in the area for five days and did a survey of the gravesites. They dug in the shell heaps hoping to find a connection to the graveyard inhabitants. They found none. When they excavated the larger ash pit, it created a hole that was eight feet across and nearly seven feet deep. The smaller ash pit excavation created a hole that was four and a half feet across by seven feet deep. No artifacts were discovered, and it was theorized that the purpose of the pits might have been a storage area for possibly corn or other food. The graves were surveyed and some more artifacts were discovered during the dig. Some of the items found are as follows: gouges (carving tools), numerous different size plummets (fishing weights), axes, and hammer stones. Mr. Moorehead stated, "That the site had been

Sullivan Falls and Sullivan Harbor

significantly compromised from 30 years earlier by the railroad construction crew." Most of the information that Moorehead gathered was from the interview he had with Mr. Milton Stratton of Hancock, Maine. Mr. Stratton lived near the excavation site during the first disturbance. He was an architect who was employed in Bar Harbor, Maine, and was locally felt to have credibility. His descendants later ran a restaurant called the Cardinal Restaurant, which was located on the Hancock side where the *Waukeag Ferry* crossed between Sullivan and Hancock. Currently, the restaurant building is operating as a mussel processing plant owned by Peter Daley.

Shortly after the Civil War, the eastern seaboard cities developed a demand for quarry stone and lumber. The materials were used for the construction of wharfs, buildings, roads, homes, and foundations. The towns of Sullivan and Franklin had a beautiful granite resource to fill the orders. Wharfs were built along Taunton, Hog and Egypt Bay to provide access for the ships to gather the stone to head to the market. By 1869, there were

Sullivan Falls and Sullivan Harbor

Present Day Gordon Wharf

Courtesy Sullivan Sorrento Historical Society

three granite quarry companies operating in Sullivan. The families of Crabtree and Clapham owned the Gordon Quarry. The Simpson family owned the Simpson Quarry. The Moore and Blaisdell families owned and operated a quarry, which the name was not listed. The owners hired teamsters to transport the stone from the quarry to the wharfs. The teamsters utilized stone-hauling wagons that were referred to as galamanders. Hay was a valuable commodity for Sullivan and Franklin teamsters. There was a great need for hay to feed all of the animals in Sullivan and Franklin areas but there was not enough pastureland to fulfill this necessity. It was not out of the ordinary for hay

Sullivan Falls and Sullivan Harbor

to be shipped to Sullivan and the schooners would export granite on their return trip.

There were several areas of Taunton Bay that offered lots of danger. Located about a half mile up

Wharf in Front of the Waukeag Mine

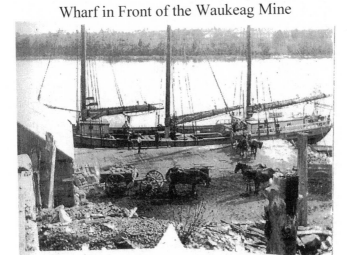

Courtesy Sullivan Sorrento Historical Society

bay from the falls, the old piers that existed from the first bridge were navigational hazards. The most dangerous part of the falls was Hatchers Rock, located above the center ledge. At times it would only be six inches below water level during low tide. This was referred to as a "sunker." On the Sullivan side, near the end of Falls Point, there were two more sunkers.

Sullivan Falls and Sullivan Harbor

During the year of 1868, schooners were lining up to enter or exit the falls to deliver their goods and load stone at the numerous wharfs. It was common to observe many vessels in Sullivan Harbor or in Taunton Bay waiting for the tides and winds. The trip through the narrow, ledge infested section known as Sullivan Falls could become a real carnival ride. Even experienced captains took heed in navigating through this area. The tides and winds had to be just right before any experienced captain would try to enter or exit the bay. During May 1868, three shipwrecks took place in the Sullivan Falls. All three ships hit sunkers near the base of the falls.

One of these wrecked vessels was the schooner *Ganges*, which was headed for New York City, New York, from Franklin, Maine. Captain Higgins was at the wheel of the127 ton, nine foot draft schooner. The *Ganges* was built in 1845 in Warren, Maine, from mixed wood with iron fasteners. The ship was owned by D. G. Eaton and called Ellsworth, Maine, its homeport. As she headed down into Frenchman's Bay, she struck the sunker

Sullivan Falls and Sullivan Harbor

Sullivan Falls Low Tide Slack
Circa 2017

Daley Collection.

at the base of the falls. She was able to float off during the next high tide. The *Ganges* was severely damaged under the stem where she lost a plank and part of her keel. She was able to limp back to a Sullivan wharf where her load was discharged and repairs were made.

The second wrecked vessel was the schooner *Wide World* that stuck the center ledge in the falls and was stranded until the next high tide. The schooner was a 251 ton vessel that was fastened with copper and iron, and framed from oak. The *Wide World* was built in Setauket, Long Island,

Sullivan Falls and Sullivan Harbor

New York, in 1854. She was owned by Jonas Smith & Company, and declared her homeport to be New York City. Captain Hilder knew that the schooner drafted 10 feet, but assumed he could clear the sunker ledges located in the falls at high tide. The *Wide World* struck the sunker and was stranded until the following high tide. The accident weakened the schooner's frame. She floated free of the ledge and successfully unloaded her cargo back at a Sullivan wharf. Due to her damage, she was deserted.

Sullivan Falls Out Going Tide
Circa 2017

Daley Collection.

Sullivan Falls and Sullivan Harbor

The third wreck was the schooner *Alice R. Bennett*, where she tore off part of her keel on a sunker next to the center ledge. The 74 ton schooner was built from mixed wood and was iron fastened. Captain Stratton was lucky the schooner only drew eight feet, because the tide was able to force her over the ledge and do only minimal damage to her keel. The *Alice R. Bennett* had been used primarily in the lumber trade and was considered a lumber coaster. In 1847, she was constructed in Eden, Maine, located on Mount Desert Island. She was owned by Captain Stratton, along with a few other business partners, and claimed Sullivan, Maine, as her homeport.

On November 19, 1868, the old piers that belonged to John Sargent's first bridge across Taunton Bay claimed the Schooner *Oregon*. The 76 ton schooner was constructed of oak with iron fasteners. She was built in 1851 in Trenton, Maine. The vessel's owner was E. Henrahan, from the homeport of Rockland, Maine. Captain Abner Gott was at the wheel when the *Oregon*, with a draft of eight feet, ran out of water. She struck the old center pier and became stranded. The collision caused her to break several planks. She was able to drift off on the next tide but quickly sank. The current raised havoc with the schooner, which was loaded with corn and flour. Finally, a crew of men was able to repair the planks, pump out the water, and raise her. The *Oregon* continued to work the shipping trade along the eastern seaboard. Disaster finally came to her off Nantucket, Massachusetts, on August 25, 1885. She was carrying granite to New Bedford when she struck a ledge on Great Point Rip, Massachusetts, and foundered on her way to Wauwinet, Massachusetts. She broke apart and rested on the shore. Locals salvaged her wood to build a summer cottage.

The business of lumber and granite had brought lucrative trade to the local areas. The Sullivan Falls was a navigational hazard which created a serious obstruction to the shipping business and claims made to insurance companies were financially unnerving. Local businessmen and politicians petitioned the government to make the waterway safer. In 1870, under the direction of the Secretary

Sullivan Falls and Sullivan Harbor

of War, they agreed to do a survey. In 1872, twenty-five thousand dollars was appropriated for needed improvements. The government wanted to remove three of the piers from the old bridge and to excavate ledges in the falls to a depth of seven feet. In 1874, an additional $3950 was raised to complete the project. About 100 cubic yards of a sunker needed to be removed to obtain the seven-foot depth required by the survey. By 1875, nearly $35,000 had been spent for improvements. This included adding two spindle markers on two different rocks near the mouth of the falls.

In 1890, a second survey and examination of the falls were authorized. An estimate of $35,000 was determined to be needed to complete the work. The survey determined that Hatchers Rock and two other points of the ledge had to be removed to a depth of ten feet. An expenditure of $9,535.31 was allotted by 1896. In 1900, it was determined that the outer end of the center ledge needed to be lowered to a depth of ten feet at mean low tide. In 1911, five thousand dollars was appropriated to finish all necessary changes. The work at the falls was complete by 1914. The greatest reason for the changes was to make it so the majority of vessels could travel safely up and down the falls at the high and low water marks. Today, larger vessels still only travel both ways within an hour before and after slack tide.

In 1883, the Sullivan Falls Tow Boat Company became incorporated. A tow boat was used to assist vessels with navigating the falls. There was a charge of six dollars for assistance each way. With the improvements in the waterway and having the choice of using a tow boat, one would surmise this

Stock Certificate, Sullivan Tow Boat Company

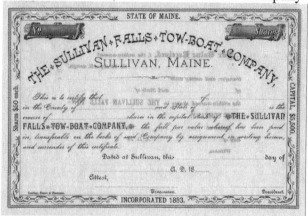

Daley Collection

stretch of water would provide safer travel, which it did. This created more traffic through the falls until roads and railways improved. In 1896, the amount of tonnage through the falls was 51,200 tons. In

Tow Boat *Phillip S. Eaton*

Courtesy Sullivan Sorrento Historical Society

1897, there were 50,790 tons. In 1898, there were 41,700 tons. In 1899, there were 42,125 tons that traversed the falls and in 1900 only 35,926 tons passed. Improvements within the railways provided safer travel for their shipments, which decreased the need for seafaring vessels.

Even with the improvements, travel through the falls remained dangerous. The disaster of the schooner *Maine* from Boston, Massachusetts, for Franklin, Maine with general merchandise, happened on November 19, 1878. The *Maine* was built in 1826 in Sullivan and was owned by Emery

& Bragdon. She was constructed of mixed wood and was fastened with iron. The vessel only drew seven feet and had been completely rebuilt in 1865. Captain Lord was at the helm when she filled with water, broke apart and sank with the shifting of the tides. Fortunately, no lives were lost.

The *Wild Rover* had been purchased in 1869 in the town of Waldoboro, Maine, and was used for trade up and down the eastern seaboard. The 63 foot, 38 ton schooner *Wild Rover* hit the ledges in Tidal Falls on July 5, 1884. She was headed into Taunton Bay to be loaded with stone. She struck the ledge and was damaged, but was able to be floated off and repaired.

On July 23, 1895, Captain Sprague was in command when his schooner, *Julia S. Bailey,* went aground at Sullivan Falls. Needless to say, Captain Sprague, was having a streak of bad luck, since this was the third vessel he had lost in a little over a year. She was a 309 ton schooner that was built in Gardner, Maine, in 1881. The Goss, Sawyer, and Packard families owned her. She was constructed from yellow pine, hardwood, and was fastened with iron and copper fasteners. The schooner was loaded with stone and was headed for Philadelphia, Pennsylvania. She struck the center ledge and remained on the ledge in a dreadful way for nearly a week. The tug, *L. A. Belknap*, came from Portland, Maine, to tow the *Julia S. Bailey* back to Portland where she would be placed in dry dock for repairs.

The schooner *Lucy Belle* was built in Columbia Falls, Maine, in 1888, and displaced 87 tons with a draft of six and a half feet. The Dunbar Brothers Company of Sullivan owned the schooner. On March 30, 1900, the *Belle* ran aground upon the center ledge of Sullivan Falls. Captain Clarence Martin decided to try to jettison half the cargo with the hope of floating the vessel on the next high tide. The ship was loaded with quarry stone headed for Boston, Massachusetts. He was able to get her afloat and with a little repair she was back in the coaster trade. Sadly, on November 30, 1901, Captain Martin struck a ledge on the southern side of Thatcher's Island, Massachusetts. Her seams opened up and she quickly sank in about 25 feet of water. The captain and crew launched a dory just in time before the ship sank. Since the vessel sank so quickly, the men were only able to save their lives. All of her cargo including the 135 tons of edge stone was lost. They rowed ashore to Rockport, Massachusetts.

The schooner *Victory* on August 29, 1901, stuck the center ledge in Sullivan Falls. She sat on the ledge during low tide and upon the next high tide she was able to float off with little damage to the keel. Her homeport was Ellsworth, Maine. She had been built in 1854 in Friendship, Maine, and completely rebuilt in 1880. The schooner was 113 ton, 89 feet long, with a breadth of 25 feet and a draft of 8½ feet. She was owned by Isaiah Blaisdell and was piloted by Captain Oldren. The *Victory* was used in the lumber, stone, and merchandise trade.

The schooner *Franconia* on September 7, 1910, was attempting to go down the falls when she struck the center ledge. She was built in 1862, in Surry, Maine, and called Ellsworth, Maine, her homeport. Captain H. Young was at the wheel when the oak framed, 129 ton vessel gave her iron fasteners a real

Sullivan Falls and Sullivan Harbor

Wreck on Sullivan Falls Center Ledge

Courtesy Sullivan Sorrento Historical Society

test. She remained there for the next six weeks. On November 16, she was floated from the ledge and moved over onto the beach at Sullivan Falls. Her bottom had been severely damaged and she had lost her keel. The vessel was repaired and later that year she was back in the seafaring trade.

The schooners would be taken to the beach below the falls for needed repairs if they were on the Frenchman's Bay's side of the ledge. The beach was a safe area to complete needed repairs for its

Sullivan Falls and Sullivan Harbor

location was in lee of the prevailing winds and out of the strong current. For years, old planks and brass spikes were discarded in this area by ships' carpenters. Once repaired the schooners would be launched by the power of oxen using block and tackle or by a tugboat.

The Sullivan Falls traffic had grown steadily as business increased above the falls. In 1878, mining came to Taunton Bay. By 1882, there were nine incorporated or privately owned mines on the Sullivan side of the bay. There were an additional twelve shafts on the Hancock and Franklin shores of Egypt, Hog, and Taunton Bays. The majority of the mining corporations were in search of copper, silver, and gold. At their peak, they employed nearly four hundred men. By 1883, the mines had started closing and by 1885, they were all nonoperational. Sporadically, some of the mines opened for short periods of time as late as 1900.

The stone quarries had reached their peak by 1890 and were employing around four hundred individuals as well. Like the mines, the stone quarries started on a downward spiral, and by 1940

Sullivan Falls and Sullivan Harbor

were no longer a large-scale employment business. They continued to sell stone but on a much smaller scale. Their downfall was caused by the advancement of reinforced concrete which lowered market demands, and costs associated with transportation and employment.

True stories as well as some exaggerated stories about the Sullivan Falls area had assisted with the promotion of this area in becoming famous. There were numerous stories within the national newspapers, in which, sea captains told legendary stories of the dangerous falls. These stories were heard across the country. Some of these stories were printed in papers as far away as California.

A story covered in a variety of papers was that of a Sullivan man by the last name of Campbell. He had become noted for his ability for birling, log rolling. He stated that he was going to ride a log through Sullivan Falls and on July 8, 1875, he attempted his feat. A large crowd gathered on both sides of falls and with nearly a 13 knot current and an eight foot wall of water he attempted to traverse the falls. Against all odds, he made it!

Sullivan Falls and Sullivan Harbor

There have been several deaths due to the incredible force of the falls. One death was on August 25, 1853. At the age of 22, Augustus Hill of Sullivan was killed in the falls when his boat upset.

Newspapers throughout America published a story about a seven-masted schooner to be built in the spring of 1901, in Franklin, Maine. Captain Frost of Franklin was to be the schooner's captain. It was investigated by several reporters and found to be not credible. The first problem was that a seven-masted schooner would never be able to pass through Sullivan Falls. Captain Frost admitted that the whole story was nothing more than a joke that had started at a local hunting camp; one might suspect there was some drinking going on at the camp.

Other financial disasters operating near the falls were some of the mines of Sullivan. One mine was the Sullivan Falls Silver Mine, which was started in the winter of 1880. It was located on what was called the Sullivan Lode across the road from what was later known as Dennis and Ruth Vibert's pottery shop on Route 1. The Sullivan Falls Silver

Sullivan Falls and Sullivan Harbor

Mine was privately owned and was allowed to sell up to 100,000 shares of stock. A. P. Wiswell was elected president, and J. B. Redman was elected secretary. They were both from Ellsworth, Maine. William H. Clapham was put in charge as superintendent of the mine. When the mine was started, a peculiar event transpired. The first miners set explosives to blast the frozen ground to create the opening for the shaft. An unbelievable amount of snakes came out of the hole below the frost line. Many perished, yet others crawled out of the debris. The snakes were green, black, yellow and even rainbow colored. This was very eerie. The mine had reached a depth of twenty feet by March of 1880. The crew built a 28 foot by 18 foot shaft house over the mine. It supposedly had a pay streak of over eight feet wide. During the operations of this mine, the shaft went below 100 feet, but the pay streak did not last. The snakes should have been a warning to all investors that this was a bad omen. This mine, like some, was a flop.

In 1887, the Sullivan Harbor Land Company was formed. It was incorporated as a resort style development. The company's CEO-elect was Amory D. Weinwright. Vice-president and general manager was Clyde D. V. Hunt. The other directors for the company were Frank Hill Smith, Dr. Morton Prince and R. N. Turnbull. The company was authorized to sell up to 100,000 shares of stock at $5 a share. This parcel of land includes parts of

Stock Certificate, Sullivan Harbor Land Company

Daley Collection

Sullivan Harbor and parts of what is now called Sorrento. The company aimed its sales towards the wealthy and prominent citizens of the time. They were hoping to recruit some of the summer crowd from Bar Harbor. The company had elaborate ideas

Sullivan Falls and Sullivan Harbor

to entice the wealthy, which included building a Moorish Lookout with a shiny dome on the top of Ossipee Mountain in Sullivan. The dome was to be covered with ten ounces of gold leaf. They hoped visitors coming by water would be impressed with such an elegant showing. The land company planned to build a causeway across Long Cove to make the two parcels of land more accessible to each other. They planned to build the road across the old gristmill located in Long Cove that was previously owned and built by the Dudley Sargent Family. The directors felt this road would make the trip shorter to the land that was located in present day Sorrento where the other portion of their land was located. When it was completed, the trip would have been one mile less and would be more appealing to potential buyers. In reality, it would not make the trip that much shorter but would, hopefully, make it a more scenic route for prospective buyers. The directors never started the construction of the road.

In March of 1889, the Sullivan Harbor Land Company was able to incorporate a second

Sullivan Falls and Sullivan Harbor

company, known as The Sullivan Harbor Water Company. It was created for the purpose of delivering drinking water to its land holdings. They were not permitted to lay pipe near Waukeag Neck, Present day Sorrento, Maine. This area was reserved for the Long Pond Water Company. The Sullivan Harbor Water Company was founded and allowed the sale of $25,000 worth of stock. An additional $75,000 worth of stock could be raised, if approved by its directors. The company was permitted to get its water from Long Pond. In 1893, the Long Pond Water Company was given the right to purchase the Sullivan Harbor Water Company for an amount that would pay off all of its outstanding bonds.

Back in July of 1891, The Sullivan Harbor Land Company received lots of publicity, which was not on the positive side. The Vice President, Clyde D. V. Hunt, was arrested for horsewhipping his wealthy brother-in-law, Francis B. Hayes. Mr. Hayes was the president of the Massachusetts Horticultural Society of Boston. He was well-known, as was Mr. Hunt, in the Sullivan and Boston areas. Mrs. Hayes decided to leave her husband because of inadequate treatment. She sued him in court and was given a legal separation and awarded $6000 a year alimony. Her brother, Mr. Hunt, became outraged with Mr. Hayes when he said some very unkind words about his ex-wife, Mrs. Hayes, to a local paper. Mr. Hunt went to the house of Mr. Hayes in Ascuteville, Windsor County, Vermont. He asked Mr. Hayes if he had authorized the insinuating statements about his sister. Mr. Hayes ran into the back room and produced a pistol, which he aimed at Mr. Hunt's head. Mr. Hunt wrestled with Mr. Hayes and was able to get the upper hand. He then took a horsewhip and gave Mr. Hayes a terrible whipping.

With the stock prices plummeting and negative press about the directors, the Sullivan Harbor Land Company was negatively affected by the economic downturn. Due to this negative publicity the Company, which had purchased large tracts of land and held interests in some of the local hotels, went defunct by 1895.

Sullivan Falls and Sullivan Harbor

A very odd event happened near the old Dudley Sargent Family Gristmill located in Sullivan Harbor in May of 1956. The story was printed in many newspapers across the United States. A late season snowstorm hit the area in which people suspected this storm may have caused disorientation in a ten foot long porpoise which became trapped behind the stone walls of the old gristmill. It is believed that due to the storm or disease the porpoise's sonar system was not working properly. Fishermen from Sullivan and Sorrento tried to lead the creature back out to sea, but to no avail. The marine mammal became stranded on shore. The porpoise became exhausted and died behind the gristmill's stone walls. The animal's carcass was later pulled up onto the bank behind George and Ruth Bartlett's store. The store was located at the head of Long Cove on the Sullivan side of the cove. The fishermen suspended the carcass from a tree for people to see and some people had their pictures taken with it. The porpoise was suspended for a couple of weeks. The creature's carcass started to smell, so it was taken down and buried in the bank near the shore. Today, the porpoise would have been identified as the Atlantic White-sided Dolphin.

Deborah and Cheryl Ashe with the Porpoise Behind Their Grandparents' Store

Courtesy of Deborah Ashe Gordon

Sullivan Falls is known as the largest reversing falls in North America. With all the stories told by the sea captains that have traversed through the falls as well as the write-ups within national newspapers, these embellished stories have added to the

37

Sullivan Falls and Sullivan Harbor

notoriety that Sullivan Falls and Sullivan Harbor have received. With such flair to the tales, one has to decipher which stories are fiction or nonfiction. It is easy to see why Sullivan Falls and Sullivan Harbor have added to the history of the sea-faring trade as well as the seafaring-trade has added to the history of this area.

Dangers of Sullivan Falls and Surrounding Bays

These areas are incredibly rich in maritime history and even today, diving and fishing in these areas can cause some serious anxiety. In Taunton Bay, we prefer to dive within an hour before and after dead low or high tide. We also have about ten minutes of what we call slack tide, little or no movement, which makes diving safer and easier. Slack tide does not exist in the middle of the falls due to the time differentials of high or low tides from Frenchman's Bay to Taunton Bay. There is

Sullivan Falls and Sullivan Harbor

about an hour and fifteen-minute difference between high or low tides above and below the falls, which means the water is constantly moving in the middle of the falls. The time difference can change depending on the flow of the tide or the amount of drain of the bay water. At one time, the falls was being considered for a location of a hydro dam. The concern for using this area was that the dam would cause the water in the bays above the falls to become warmer due to restricting how much flow would transpire. This would cause destruction to the marine life that flourishes throughout the upper bays.

Howard "Tomcat" Gordon gave John some advice on how to navigate the falls, "Be damn careful and if you're in doubt, don't go!" John thought, "Wow, I have heard a lot of stories from my dad and others about how dangerous this place could be. Since Tomcat had fished these waters for over fifty years and he was afraid of them, then I had better be as well, or it was going to be one short fishing career." John learned of certain obstructions in the falls, the speed of the currents and how the hydraulics and eddies would shift the boat. It can be best described as a place you have to learn by experience and not a place where anyone can verbally teach you how to navigate. At dead slack tide, one can traverse through the falls without much difficulty.

During the time we have fished and dived in this area, we have had to assist or rescue numerous individuals who have found themselves in terrible predicaments. In 2014, Bruce Munger of the Sullivan Fire Department asked us to document some of our involvement with rescues from the dangerous waters of Taunton Bay. We have participated in at least six cases, in which we have helped to rescue ten people in distress.

One rescue was when a husband and wife rolled their canoe in Sullivan Falls. They were staying at Island View Inn in Sullivan Harbor and were coming up over the falls on an incoming tide. They rolled and were clinging to their canoe as we spotted them going under the old Sullivan Singing Bridge. We sailed our old 20 foot Eastport Lobster Boat alongside them. They were as happy as

Sullivan Falls and Sullivan Harbor

singing larks to have us pull them aboard. We were able to drain their canoe and transport it over the falls. The man asked us to please let him and his wife back into their canoe near Edgewater Inn. John asked him why they would not want us to drop them off at the town landing next to Island View Inn. He said it would be too embarrassing for him since his brother-in-law had warned him not to go near the falls. John told him, he was going to have to tell his brother-in-law that they went swimming because their clothes were soaked. He laughed and said they would row around awhile and hope that the sun would dry their clothes.

Another rescue involved Philip Stroup, John's stepfather/sternman, and John. While they were lobster fishing below the falls on the Hancock side, they spotted two people in kayaks near Tidal Falls. A man in his forties and a ten years old boy were out for some fun. As John was pulling a trap, they heard someone yell, "Help!" They saw the man swimming next to his kayak in the cold water and the young boy paddling towards the man trying to save him. John was afraid that if they did not reach them quickly that the two of them may both end up in the water. John dropped the trap and steered the boat over to them. If the little boy rolled his kayak, it would no longer be a one person rescue. John yelled for the young fellow to move away and let them attend to the man. After pulling up next to the man Phil and John grabbed him by his lifejacket and bobbed him in the water to lift him aboard their boat. Then they tended to his kayak by pulling it onboard and draining it. The man stated he lost his wallet from his pocket during his struggle when his kayak flipped. He was fortunate he did not lose his car keys. He had secured them in a dry pouch and had attached the dry pouch to his hip. He stated, since he was thoroughly soaked and upset about losing his wallet, he was done kayaking for the day.

One early morning our uncle, Robert Havey, called John to report that he saw an upside-down boat in the bay. He said he saw it go under the Sullivan Bridge on the incoming tide. John hung up and told Marlene to get ready. The phone rang again and it was the Maine State Police dispatcher calling. He stated a 911 call had come into the office. He knew we lived by the bridge and had immediate access to a boat. He asked if we would hurry out into the bay for a boater was in distress. John responded, "Marlene and I are on our way." When we boarded our boat, we headed up bay. We spotted an upside down white tri-hull boat floating in the current in the middle of the bay. A man was sitting on the hull. We approached the man and he told us to forget him and rescue his son-in-law and grandson. He said he was alright but was worried about his son-in-law and grandson who had been in the boat with him. The son-in-law was swimming with the grandson in tow towards the beach at the shore of Gordon Cemetery. Dr. Chris Mace and his wife Suzanne were waiting for them with a blanket. The man said they were fine and to please help his father-in-law. Upon our return to the upside down boat, we were able to help the gentleman from his boat and onto our boat. Donnie Tozier of Hancock and Chris Briggs of Sullivan arrived with their boats after hearing via the CB about an upside down craft in Taunton Bay. They were able to right his boat and tow it to Gordon's Wharf. The gentleman told

Sullivan Falls and Sullivan Harbor

us that he had anchored his boat below the bridge. He had tied his anchor line to the back of his boat. They were fishing and the tide started to run hard. He went to the back of the boat and tried to pull his anchor, but could not break it loose. The boat filled with water, capsized and begun to roll in the current. The grandson, who was wearing a life jacket, was caught inside the boat as it rolled. The grandson popped out when the anchor line broke. They were carried up bay by the current. Maine State Marine Warden, Michael Pinkham, was waiting at Gordon's Wharf to discuss the incident when we dropped the gentleman off.

A fourth rescue took place one early afternoon while we were working at the Galley Restaurant. A woman came running into the restaurant and asked if John could save her sister to whom she was talking with via cell phone. She informed us they had been kayaking in the bay and that her sister was beached in Sullivan Falls, "on the island." We believed the "island" to be the center ledge. We boarded our lobster boat and headed to the center ledge, but could not find her. We asked people at

Sullivan Falls and Sullivan Harbor

Tidal Falls Picnic Area if they had seen anyone kayaking. They said there were people up above the falls earlier kayaking but had not seen them for a while. We went above the falls and spotted her sitting on a rock at Falls Point with her kayak. She was very glad to accept a ride and said she did not want to leave this island via kayak due to being afraid of the current taking her out to sea. We informed her she was not on an island, but on the upper side of Falls Point.

A fifth rescue took place when John, was fishing under the Sullivan Bridge. John spotted a man in his forties in the water next to a tiny 12 foot sailboat. The man, once rescued, stated to John that he had been down by the opening of the falls when he flipped the sailboat. The current had rolled him out of his boat and carried the sailboat and him up bay. John was able to get his sailboat drained and assisted him back into it. John asked him if he knew this area he was trying to sail was very dangerous. John noticed the man did not have a lifejacket on, so John mentioned to him that he should be wearing a lifejacket. He said that he had a lifejacket inside his boat. John informed him that he definitely should put it on because it does not provide any floatation for him being inside the boat. He informed John that he was from New Jersey and that he was an experienced sailor. John had his doubts. The sailor was very grateful, but he seemed not to have a full understanding of the dangerous current. He sailed off toward Burying Island and John sailed off to pick up Philip Stroup. They were hauling lobster traps for around two hours, when Marlene waived them in to shore. Marine Warden, Michael Pinkham, was waiting for them with Marlene on the landing on the Sullivan side at the base of the Sullivan Bridge. Warden Pinkham informed them that he had received a call from a Maine State Dispatcher that a family reported there was a small sailboat and its owner overdue. John told him that, earlier in the day, he had already rescued this sailor once. Warden Pinkham wanted us to assist in helping him find the fellow. We motored up bay and after about two miles spotted the sailor near the Hancock shore. He was in the water pumping the water out of his sailboat before attempting to board. John advised Warden Pinkham that the man was not someone who came across as belligerent, but as a confused individual, who did not understand the dangers of the bay. Warden Pinkham stated he would judge that once he had met him. We pulled up alongside of him. Warden Pinkham called him by name and informed him he had been sent out to look for him. The sailor stated that he was fine. Warden Pinkham asked, "Where is your lifejacket?" The sailor answered, "I have one inside my boat." Warden Pinkham informed him to wear it. The sailor did not have one; all he had was a seat cushion. Warden Pinkham took one of John's lifejackets and had him wear it. They hooked a line to his boat and towed him into Egypt Bay, where he was camping with some of his relatives. Warden Pinkham had a long talk with him and his relatives about safety concerns and the dangers of the bay.

A sixth rescue happened on our daughter Jessie's, 13th Birthday, November 7, 1999. During this time, the Singing Bridge was being dismantled and replaced. A number of coincidences had to occur for this rescue to have been successful. It was a Sunday and we had taken our daughters out for breakfast. We planned to attend the turkey shoots sponsored by the Franklin Veterans Club, but it started to rain and the turkey shoots were canceled. That morning, we bought gas for the lobster boat and picked up a new doorknob for our front door. Due to the cancellation of the turkey shoot, we went home. John put the boat gas in the shed and started working on replacing the door knob. We owned a beautiful yellow lab by the name of Susie. She was always on the lobster boat and swam continuously in Taunton Bay. John was trying to adjust the new doorknob and was testing how it worked by repeatedly opening and shutting the door. Susie came up to the step and started barking at him. John assumed she was barking because of the noise created by the opening and shutting of the door. John told her to shut up and get out of his way. She went to the shore and returned a few minutes later and continued barking. John did notice that she was wet and had been swimming. It was a cold day and had been snowing earlier, but it was not unusual for

Sullivan Falls and Sullivan Harbor

Susie to be in the water. John hollered at her and said, "Get out of here!" Then, he slammed the door and went inside to watch the football game.

About fifteen minutes later, Ronald Stanley of Gouldsboro, Maine, pulled in the yard yelling for help. John ran out and saw Ronald standing outside of his van. He yelled to John and asked if he had a boat. John said yes and asked why. Ronald stated that while crossing the bridge he had looked down into the water and noticed an older man popping up out of a whirlpool. He saw the man struggling in the middle of the bay about 20 minutes ago. When asked what took him so long to come to us to acquire assistance, he replied that he went to see Tomcat Gordon for help, but he was not home. Ronald attempted to start Tomcat's boat but was unsuccessful. John quickly retrieved his gas from the shed and we hurried to our boat. It was moored in the cove in front of the house. The tide was running hard up the bay. We went to the center of the bay and scooted along, scanning both sides of the shore. We were almost to Burying Island when we noticed something moving in the water next to a buoy. As we approached, John recognized the object as a human head and yelled to him, "Are you alone?" The man did not respond. John screamed at him for fear there might be others in the water. The floating man finally answered and said that he was alone. We pulled up next to him; John and Marlene lifted him up over the side and sat him in the bottom of the boat. His legs were of little use to him since he was suffering from hypothermia. The man was obviously blind in one eye and stated he lost his glasses. He was confused and quite emotional. He asked John if he knew where his glasses were. John said, "I have no idea." The man then told us that his wife was right. She said that he was a damn old fool. He then told us that he owned two homes, one was a cottage on Taunton Bay in Hancock and the other home was in Frenchman's Bay on Hancock Point. He described his cottage on Taunton Bay and John knew where it was. It was about one mile away. We felt it was most important to get him warm and he told us he had heat available in his cottage so we headed to his cottage. He asked John to save his small sculling boat. John

Sullivan Falls and Sullivan Harbor

did not want to waste time, but the elderly man was so insistent on retrieving the little boat that John grabbed it and drained the water out. John quickly threw it across the bow of the boat to assist with calming the man's emotions. John was even able to retrieve his small oars. The man was only wearing a white sweater and pair of shorts, which was not appropriate for the time of year or weather. He did not have a lifejacket on, but there was one in his boat. This was what allowed the tip of his little boat to stay afloat. Ronald lay down beside the man trying to keep him warm, while John drove the boat to the shore near the man's home. Once there, we assisted him out of the boat and up the set of steps that led to his cottage. John and Ronald went in and assisted him into a warm shower. He gave Marlene his wife's phone number so she could call her. He said his wife would give him a ride to the Maine Coast Memorial Hospital, Ellsworth, ME. Once she arrived, we left.

We never saw the man again until Christmas Eve. Famous for being last minute shoppers, it was noontime and we were in our bedroom secretly

51

discussing what more we wanted to buy for our daughters for Christmas. We heard a knock at the front door, and shortly thereafter, our daughter Jessie came into our bedroom. She said there was a man who wanted to talk to us. John went out and saw the man. He looked to be in his 70's and was well dressed in a suit and a tie. John's first thought was that the man was a Jehovah's Witness making a visit. The older man spoke first and asked, "You have no idea who I am, do you?" John said, "You are correct." He said, "I am the man you saved from the bay. My name is William Peake. I have been asking people about you and they tell me you're not the kind of man to take money for saving my life. But I want you to have this for collecting my boat and oars." He handed John a large white thick envelope. John laughed and thought that if it had not been a serious moment, he would have said, "Tell me who is telling lies about me!"

Mr. Peake then went on and told John what actually happened. He said that he was sculling in the bay when he neared the pilings of the old

Sullivan Falls and Sullivan Harbor

bridgework. He heard our dog, Susie, bark and he turned to look. Just as he turned to see Susie, he

Susie

Daley Collection

saw a beam hanging down that was about to hit him in the back of his head. He ducked and rolled his boat over. He said he was lucky the dog warned him. If the dog had not barked, he would have been knocked out. He then said after rolling out of the boat, he started swimming at this point he had to decide to swim for shore or stay with his little craft. Susie swam out to him, barked, and swam around him. He did not understand that she had played a swimming game with the family many times in Flanders Pond. She would swim around us and one of us would grab her hind end which she would pull us to shore. Susie returned one more time to Mr. Peake, but he chose to stay with his boat. John told him how lucky he was and that God had somehow decided to save him. He laughed and said, "I was afraid God had forgotten me." John said, "Oh no, he sent my dog, Susie, out to you twice and then finally me." Mr. Peake thanked us again before leaving. Inside the envelope, there was an L.L. Bean catalog and a gift certificate for $100.00. Coincidentally, it was the only place still open in Ellsworth on Christmas Eve. We bought the girls a sled and a dog bed for Susie. A lot of occurrences had to coincide for this rescue to have been successful. If the order of events had changed, the gentleman may not have survived.

Sullivan Falls is a treacherous area. The current runs very strong in this spot. The crevices and shipwrecks in this area provide a great location for catching food and locating artifacts. If traps are situated in the right place, within Tidal Falls, they can catch some beautiful big lobsters. Tomcat used to tell a story of a huge lobster living in the falls. He stated that a diver was untangling gear in the

Sullivan Falls and Sullivan Harbor

falls when he saw a lobster he claimed to be as big as a man.

Many times our warps lines from the traps to the buoys, would become entangled and would not break loose. This led us to dive in this location in hopes of determining what was holding the warps. We asked a couple of divers to assist us in investigating the area. Friends and fellow divers, Royce Gordon and Randy Mosley agreed to dive the area. Sure enough, Randy followed down one of the entangled lines and found that it led to an old anchor. A plan was formulated to use a homemade lift bag to bring the anchor to the surface. If successful, the anchor would be preserved. PADI Divemaster, Mark Andrews, of Sullivan was recruited to assist. Mark is an excellent diver and auto mechanic who is always up for an adventure. To construct the lift bag, Mark and John used an old salmon cage net and put a large skidder inner tube inside it. They dove at low tide in about 25 feet of water. They had approximately 12 minutes to complete the task. One of the anchor's flukes was sticking straight up from the bottom and the other was buried in the rocky boulders of the bottom. It had a large metal ring that passed through its eye. This indicated that the anchor was secured by rope and not by chain. The anchor originally had a wooden stock, which had deteriorated and was no longer present. Since there was a wooden stock, this indicated the anchor was constructed before 1850. After 1850, anchors were fabricated with metal stocks. It may have been a deck anchor but due to the wooden stock it most likely hung over the side with the stock resting against the side of the boat. During rough seas, they would attempt to bring it aboard. They noticed the shaft was slightly bent. This indicates that the anchor had been under a tremendous amount of force at one point. Mark and John fastened the homemade lift bag around the throat and crown of the anchor. They used a pressure hose connected to a scuba tank to inflate the tube. Once inflated, the anchor never moved! The current started to increase in intensity causing them to leave the lift bag attached to the anchor. During the incoming tide that night, the homemade lift bag was ripped from the anchor. The next day, they found it floating free in the upper bay. James West of Sorrento had a large mussel dragger and agreed to lift the anchor. His vessel was equipped with winches. Mark and John wrapped a half-inch chain around the anchor to the shackle and steel cable. At high tide, James was able to winch the anchor and leave it on the beach in Sorrento, ME.

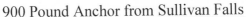
900 Pound Anchor from Sullivan Falls

Daley Collection

When the tide was low, the anchor was retrieved via a pickup and a preservation process was started. When recovered objects made of iron that have been submerged in saltwater, they need an electrolysis bath. Due to an electrolysis bath being time consuming and expensive, John chose a cheaper process of leaving the relic in fresh water for a year, hence the anchor found a home in a small stream. After removing it from the stream, oil and a hot top sealant were applied to slow the deterioration process.

Taunton Bay Crossings

A ferry to cross Taunton Bay was started by Revolutionary War Hero, Paul Dudley Sargent, in 1788. Shortly after the end of the Revolutionary War, he moved his family to Sullivan, Maine, from Boston, Massachusetts. Prior to the war, he owned many shares in sea going vessels that were used for shipping up and down the east coast as well as to Europe. He had accumulated a relatively large fortune through shipping before the war. During the American Revolution, he financially funded a military company of nearly 200 men to fight for freedom. He was given the title of Colonel and led his men in some famous battles. Colonel Sargent was wounded at Bunker Hill and crossed the Delaware with General Washington. Paul became ill after three years and went back to his home to recuperate. He decided to invest in American privateering. He owned and funded some of the most successful privateers of the American Revolution. In a famous sea battle, Paul's 80 ton privateer, *Yankee,* took on the much larger 300 ton, British merchant vessel, *Zachariah Bayley.* The *Bayley* was captured and converted into a successful privateer known as the *Boston*.

Colonel Paul Dudley Sargent

Courtesy University of Maine Collection

After moving his family to Sullivan, Colonel Sargent, age 44, was greatly in debt. Because of the expenses he had incurred during the war, he was almost bankrupt. His debt was accumulated from a combination of funding his fellow soldiers as well as from the losses he incurred from the British privateers robbing his ships. He applied for and was granted a military pension, but it was later taken from him on the pretense that he was too rich to receive one. He was appointed as the Hancock County Court Judge and later removed from this position due to being charged with willful and corrupt extortion. The case was lacking evidence on the actual justification for dismissal. He was not allowed to speak on his own behalf during the trial at the Supreme Court of Hancock County and was convicted. The charge was that Judge Sargent had over penalized a citizen three dollars on a fine.

Senator John Quincy Adams stated, because of his outstanding revolutionary and patriotic commitment, Colonel Sargent deserved to speak on his behalf. Even with Senator Adam's support, Colonel Sargent was not allowed to speak. He chose to resign due to the controversy. The Massachusetts Legislature refused Judge Sargent's resignation, but later the resignation was accepted by the Governor.

Colonel Sargent's first business adventure in Sullivan was to run a ferry across Taunton Bay. He applied and was granted sole rights for a ferry. This was his only means of making a living. He needed the income to support his wife and eleven children.

Taunton Bay Crossings

The Colonel was able, with the ferry, to barely make ends meet.

In 1821, the State of Maine granted his son, John Sargent, the exclusive right to build a bridge at the ferry's location. The ferry's schedule was contingent on the current and the tide, which made it difficult for the residents. A bridge would make the crossing more convenient for all travelers. John Sargent and his associates were incorporated as "Proprietors of Sullivan Bridge." They were provided with the ownership to hold the sole right in crossing this waterway with a bridge. In 1823, the first Sullivan Bridge was finished.

During 1823, Colonel Sargent again petitioned the U.S. Government for a pension. He was in debt and owed more than his home was worth. He was required to give a detailed list of his real estate property as well as his personal property to the government. The government finally agreed to give him twenty dollars a month. This would be about $460 per month in 2017. He started receiving his pension at the ripe old age of 81 and died two years later.

Taunton Bay Crossings

The bridge had been assembled from wooden cribs filled with rocks, and a deck made of spruce plank with railings placed on both sides. In the center of the bridge, a draw was constructed with a distance of twenty-four feet. Ships were allowed to go through the draw at no charge. The bridge had to be high enough for small boats to pass under due to not wanting to have to raise the draw. Raising the draw would inconvenience the travelers using the bridge for passage. The bridge charged tolls to cross.

The tolls for crossing the bridge in 1823, were as follows:

- A sheep or swine, three cents
- A person, twelve and a half cents
- A horse or cattle without a rider, sixteen cents
- A rider and one horse, thirty-five cents
- A sleigh or carriage drawn by one horse, fifty cents
- A carriage or sleigh with two horses, eighty cents

- A carriage drawn by four horses, one dollar
- The toll charge was ten cents cheaper if beasts, such as oxen, drew the sleigh or carriage.

There were limits as to how many animals could be moved across the bridge at one time. There could not be more than ten in a herd and at no time could one herd be closer than 100 feet to the other.

Sadly, 200 feet of the bridge was destroyed on April 2, 1829. During an early spring thaw, a heavy amount of ice from Egypt and Hog Bays destroyed the bridge as it passed through Taunton Bay. The proprietors were never able to raise the finances needed to structurally secure the bridge again. The Sargent family continued to run a ferry after the loss of the bridge. The previous ferry ran from Sullivan to Sullivan. On February 2, 1828, the town of Hancock was created from portions of the towns of Sullivan and Trenton. The Sullivan Ferry now went between two towns, Sullivan and Hancock.

On March 9, 1836, the Maine Legislature authorized the corporate group known as, "Franklin Bridge Proprietors." They were given the sole right for the next five years to construct a bridge over Taunton Bay. They could choose to place the bridge anywhere between John West's land in Sullivan and Levi Clark's land in Franklin. The group, also, had the right to choose the same location of the previous bridge in 1823. A survey would be completed to determine the best place for the bridge's location. This group was unable to accumulate the needed funds to construct a bridge.

In 1846, nineteen local citizens met to discuss building a bridge. On June 19th, the Maine Legislature agreed to the incorporation of a group known as the "Sullivan Bridge." They would now have the sole right to build a toll bridge across Taunton Bay and were given six years to complete the bridge. The legislature set forth the following restrictions for the cooperation: if someone was going to a funeral, on military duty, going to church, or if the attendant at the bridge was absent, it was free to cross. The corporation, Sullivan Bridge, was unable to acquire enough funding to build a bridge.

On February 8, 1867, Hancock resident, Ransom

B. Abbott, was given the right by the Maine Legislature to establish and maintain a ferry between Sullivan and Hancock. The ferry was propelled by the tides with one or two oarsmen. Ransom was allowed to build and maintain needed landings and to store necessary equipment to run a

Waukeag Ferry

Courtesy Sullivan Sorrento Historical Society

successful ferry on both sides of the bay. He was given rights to the land 100 feet southeast of the old bridge abutments on the Hancock and Sullivan sides. Mr. Abbott charged 40 cents for a carriage, one horse, and up to two passengers. A double team cost 50 cents. A foot passenger was charged ten cents and any additional animals were 15 cents apiece. The first single horse or oxen, was charged

Taunton Bay Crossings

25 cents. Swine and sheep were eight cents apiece.

In 1875, Ransom B. Abbott and his associates, known as the "Sullivan and Hancock Steam Ferry Company," were granted the rights to run the ferry for an additional 20 years. As it was much too dangerous, the ferry did not run during extreme weather. In 1887, Ransom "Ernest" Abbot had a cable strung across the bay. It was rigged with pulleys and had the tide as the propelling power.

Waukeag Ferry
(Bottom right ferry cable and the large building on the right across the bay is the Milton Silver Mine)

Courtesy Sullivan Sorrento Historical Society

The cable was galvanized and was 2 ¼ inches thick. It weighed 1100 pounds and was 1270 feet long. The cable had a certified strength of 20 ton. If the tide was running hard, a crossing could be made in two and a half minutes. The company now would be able to cross at more convenient times and not worry quite so much about the strong tides. The whirlpools that the ferry would travel through would cause it to sway back and forth. On one of these occasions, the ferry was crossing and a merchant by the name of Jake Altman and his horse were thrown overboard. He was scared to death. After making it safely to shore, he retold the story many times.

In April of 1919, Bradbury Smith of Sullivan was given the sole right to run a ferry over the waters of Taunton Bay by the Maine State Legislature. No one was allowed to run a ferry within one mile of his landing. He held these rights from 1921 to February 15, 1931. He was authorized to lay a cable across the waterway on the bottom so not to obstruct any vessel traffic. The cable would be lifted by the ferry as the ferry traveled across the bay. The cable would make the trip safer and allow for a more consistent schedule. A motorized scow would push the ferry from one side to the other. The name of the venture was the

Taunton Bay Crossings

Waukeag Ferry. Oddly, the prices charged by Mr.

Advertisement for Waukeag Ferry

WAUKEAG FERRY - - - West Sullivan, Maine

On the trunk line to the Provinces.
(Follow the Blue Line)
Direct route from Bangor, Ellsworth, and Bar Harbor to Sullivan,
Sorrento, Winter Harbor, Milbldge, Machias, and all points East.
Ten miles from Ellsworth.

BRADBURY SMITH, Prop.   Telephone 3108

Daley Collection

Smith were slightly lower in some cases than those charged in 1867. A passenger on foot was only five cents and a car cost its owner one dollar to cross.

Motorized Scow Used for Propulsion

Courtesy Sullivan Sorrento Historical Society

Mr. Smith was required by his contract with the Maine State Legislature to transport freight from the ferry to the Waukeag Train Station for a standard set fee. The hours of operation were set from May 15 until September 15 from five in the morning until nine at night. The rest of the year it ran from sunrise until seven at night. The ferry crossed seven

Waukeag Train Station Hancock

Courtesy Sullivan Sorrento Historical Society

days a week unless inclement weather prevented safe passage. Also, it had to be available to run if a train stopped at the railroad station. In 1918, Harvey Thomas and Gilman Martin were hired to help Bradbury Smith's crew maintain a regular schedule. Mr. Smith had to pay a penalty if passengers were made to wait an unreasonable amount of time. Due to this penalty, the ferry waited on the Hancock side for that was the location of the train station. The people on the Sullivan side would complain, but to no avail. A signal was given, such as blowing a horn, if someone on the

Waukeag Ferry Motorized Scow Carrying Three Cars

Courtesy Sullivan Sorrento Historical Society

Sullivan side wanted to cross. Mr. Smith's ferry was under the supervision of the Hancock County Commissioners. At any time the commissioners felt that Mr. Smith was not living up to his charter, they could force a sale of the ferry by eminent domain.

On April 5, 1921, the Maine State Legislature passed an act to raise money to build a Sullivan Bridge. In the same act, they acknowledged the need to pay restitution for damages suffered to the owners of the Waukeag Ferry. The damages suffered were loss of revenue and loss of the necessity for the equipment. The act stated that a fair amount would be set aside from the joint construction fund to pay Mr. Bradbury Smith and

Sullivan Bridge and the Waukeag Ferry
(on the left, deserted ferry)

Courtesy Sullivan Sorrento Historical Society

his associates. On May 14, 1926, the Waukeag Ferry Association filed a petition with the county commissioners to determine the damages suffered. Public travel was started over the Hancock Sullivan Bridge on May 17, 1926. This ended the ferry service.

On July 19, 1926, a hearing was held to determine the amount of money to be paid to the association for damages. The association wanted to be paid for its prospective loss of profits, tolls, and revenues from May 1926 until the end of their charter, which was February 15, 1931. The commissioners wanted to include the diminished value of the boats because of use and age. The final compensation was ordered from the court and the commissioners were told to come up with a fair and appropriate value. The Waukeag Ferry Association was told they had the right to sell their equipment for more than the set price the county commissioners had offered. If they were not able to sell in a reasonable time frame, they would need to take the offer from the county. On September 25, 1926, the Waukeag Ferry Association held an auction in Sullivan for its equipment. They were able to sell some of the equipment, but the large ferry was not sold. They listed a 45 horsepower Frisbee engine on a motorboat, a 25 horsepower motorboat built by the Camden Anchor & Rockland Machine Company, and two scows suitable for lighters or some other purposes. The ferry was about 50 feet long by 12 feet wide and was used during the construction of the steel bridge. It was later deserted on the shore in Hancock near its landing. In the 1940's and through the 1950's, the ferry remained on the shore and on many occasions Raymond Daley and Clarence Ashe of Sullivan would play on it and remove old pieces of iron and brass to sell to the junk dealer. Two possibilities were rumored about the remains of the ferry. People believe the ferry either rotted away on the shore or that the ice from the upper bays may have dragged it into Taunton Bay. The old landing for the ferry on the Hancock shore is south of the bridge and the Sullivan landing was located on the shore in front of The Galley Restaurant. The remains of the landings consist of stone and old timbers protruding from the shoreline and they are still visible.

The first surface of the Sullivan Bridge was concrete. It was later removed due to being too slippery. Metal grates replaced the concrete. The Sullivan Bridge became known to many as the "Singing Bridge" due to the noise made by the tires on the metal grates. Motorcyclist had difficulty with the grates because it would make their tires feel unstable as that drove over the bridge. The middle of the bridge turned on a track on the center piling powered by a Model T Engine. This allowed

Sullivan Bridge – "Singing Bridge"

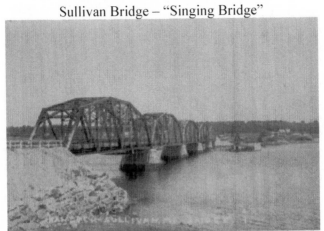

Courtesy Sullivan Sorrento Historical Society

the bridge to open so vessel could pass. There were two stone abutments on each side of the center of the bridge. These were ship deflectors. Locals referred to the abutments as ice breakers because as the ice would strike the deflectors during the spring thaw they would break the ice into smaller sections.

Today, the old "Singing Bridge" has been torn down. Reed and Reed Construction, of Woolwich, Maine built a modern 1010 foot long bridge, which is 50 feet wide. The bridge consists of drilled shaft and seven H-pile foundations with precast concrete girders. The structure was completed in October of

1999. The old bridge remains were removed over

Removing Old Sullivan Bridge

Daley Collection

the next year. The new bridge does not sing and many people have stated how they miss hearing the old bridge sing.

Searching for the Waukeag Ferry

For over 30 years, we have lobster fished and made numerous dives in this area of the bay. It was rumored the Waukeag Ferry was deserted on the Hancock shore just south of the present day bridge. John talked with his uncle, Raymond Daley and

Taunton Bay Crossings

Clarence Ashe on numerous occasions about the location of the old ferry's remains and their description never varied. Finding the old Hancock landing was easy.

In 2011, we taught an Underwater Archeology Class at the University of Maine at Machias (UMM). One of the days of diving was set aside to look for the remains of the old ferry. If artifacts were located, we would preserve them and place those artifacts on display at the Sullivan Sorrento Historical Society.

In August of that year, we had two students dive on the Hancock side of Taunton Bay about 700 feet south of the bridge. The divers were twin brothers, Kevin and Keith VanGorden from New Hampshire. They were 22 years old and were Advanced Open Water certified divers through the Professional Association of Diving Instructors (PADI). Being identical twins, wearing black wet suits, and having masks covering their faces, it was difficult to know which one we were conversing with during the dive. We started the dive a little past slack on the incoming tide. This would provide the best possible visibility. We were able to continuously monitor their whereabouts by having each diver carry a line attached to a buoy. Both students rolled out of the dive boat, which was a 20 foot Corson with a 140 horse-power Tohatsu Engine. John was in charge of the boat and Marlene was the safety diver for this dive. John's step-father, Philip Stroup, was aboard helping with the logistics, such as keeping record of dive times. After the dive, they reported their deepest depth was about 15 feet and when they first landed on the bottom, the contour was a bed of sea grass. As they continued the dive, they noticed the bottom was very flat and had little relief. It consisted of mud, clamshells, sea cucumbers, and kelp. They reported the visibility to be about ten feet. During the thirty-minute dive, they found two old bottles and a broken piece of pottery. They were unable to retrieve anything that could be identifiable or related to the old ferry. We believe there may be remains present, but are probably buried in the soft mud near the old Hancock landing. We plan at a later date to run another field school and search again for remains of the ferry.

Crabtree Ledge Lighthouse

On August 4, 1884, U.S. Congress appropriated money to construct a lighthouse to be erected on Crabtree Ledge. The ledge is located about one quarter of a mile off-shore from Hancock Point. In 1889, construction began and on January 15, 1890, the lighthouse went into service. Crabtree Ledge Lighthouse cost $38,000 to build. It was, also, needed as a guide to assist traffic traveling in this area. Traffic heading for Taunton, Egypt, and Hog Bays would have to pass through Frenchmen's Bay. All ferries that traveled to the Mount Desert Ferry Terminal at Hancock Point benefitted from the safety this light provided. The Maine Central Railroad operated a rail line to the ferry. The lighthouse was constructed on a submerged ledge, which was about three feet under normal low tide and was referred to as a sunker. It was an incredibly hazardous location for vessels. The lighthouse was constructed primarily of cast iron and brick. The brick and mortar was used to create a flat base for the lighthouse. A circular caisson went up from the base of the ledge to 32 feet. This caisson section was made of cast iron and was 25

Crabtree Ledge Lighthouse

Crabtree Ledge Lighthouse
Circa before 1903

Courtesy US Coast Guard (Historical)

feet in diameter with a 2 inch thickness at the base. On top of this section, another caisson was set. It was only 20 feet in diameter and was approximately 10 feet high. The third caisson was 18 feet in diameter and about 15 feet high. The fourth caisson was about 10 feet in diameter and about 8 feet high. The remaining section of the structure was 8 feet in diameter and about 8 feet high. The complete structure rose 73 feet from the base of the ledge to the top of the ventilator ball.

Crabtree Ledge Lighthouse

The top section of the lighthouse held the light and most of the mechanical apparatus. The focal plane was 48.5 feet above mean high water. A fifth-order polygonal Fresnel lens flashed every 1 minute and 48 seconds for a 12-second durational flash. The lens was constructed by Paris H. Lepaute. The flash was created by panels, which circulated around the lens. An iron clock table using a system of weights determined the time and duration of the flash. The lighthouse light source was fueled by lamp oil. Surrounding the outside of

Crabtree Ledge Lighthouse
Circa 1910

Courtesy U.S. Coast Guard (Historical)

Crabtree Ledge Lighthouse

the lens were eight sections of ¼ inch glass plates. These windowpanes measured 34 inches by 36 inches. The upper or third balcony was near the windows and had two rails on its platform that encircled the lighthouse. The second balcony being just below the third balcony had a lightning spindle attached to its deck and extended beyond the top balcony. The first or lower balcony had three railings that went all the way around the lighthouse for safety. On the lower balcony, there were two sets of steps leading down to the water. The two sets of stairs were positioned on opposite sides of the lighthouse to make entering or exiting the lighthouse safer. This made the access available to people contingent on the current and weather. In 1891, a 1,200 pound mechanical bell was attached to the cylindrical foundation pier on the first deck. The lighthouse was originally painted brown, but in 1903 was changed to white.

Inside the lighthouse, a circular set of stairs spiraled all the way to the top. Inside the caisson below the bottom deck, a cistern system was put in place. It collected all of the rainwater from the roof.

Crabtree Ledge Lighthouse

A coal stove provided heating for the living quarters. With a coal bin placed in the lowest section. The lighthouse keepers' beds were on the third floor.

The first lighthouse keeper was Charles Chester. He was originally from Philadelphia. He possessed

Keeper Charles F. Chester and Wife Mary Ellen Chester

Courtesy Hancock Historical Society

a very extensive maritime resume. He had been at sea since the age of 11 and was a captain of a ship at the early age of 19. Charles was married to Mary

Crabtree Ledge Lighthouse

Ellen Blake and they had 11 children. Captain Chester was the lighthouse keeper until 1908.

Death came to the little lighthouse on October 2, 1916. Light Keeper Jerome H. Peasley was ill with pneumonia and the Assistant Light Keeper, 30 year old Chester Brinkworth, was placed in charge. He hired his 18 year old brother Leon to assist him. Toward evening, Leon had gone ashore to pick up some supplies. He returned to the lighthouse with his groceries. The weather had been stormy and the water rough. It is only a guess as to what transpired at this point. The groceries were still in the dory and the table was set for supper. It is believed that Leon fell into the water and screamed to his brother for help. Chester, it is assumed, saw his brother in trouble and jumped from the lighthouse to the dory, which was adrift. He passed through the bottom of the dory, hitting his chin and breaking his jaw, which knocked him unconscious. The following day, residents on Hancock Point noticed that the light was still lit. Since it was a bright and clear day, a group went to the lighthouse to investigate.

That afternoon, a young boy found the

Crabtree Ledge Lighthouse

lighthouse dory full of water with a hole in it big enough for a man to pass through. The oars were stowed in proper position with the painter dragging in the water. Two days later, Inspector C. E. Sherman aboard Lighthouse Tender, *Hibiscus,* from Portland joined in the search. An uncle to the boys, George E. Moon and his friend Ora Jordan of Hancock began to grapple near the lighthouse. About 30 feet from the base of the lighthouse the body of Chester was located and recovered. Two days later using the same method, the two men recovered Leon, the younger brother, approximately 100 feet from the lighthouse. An autopsy was performed by the medical examiner, Dr. Hodgkins of Ellsworth, Maine, which indicated that Chester had a broken jaw.

Ora Jordan later became the keeper of the lighthouse. Six months later in 1917, tragedy came to Crabtree Ledge one more time when assistant light keeper Captain Joseph Whitmore drowned on his way out to the lighthouse. There were numerous keepers and assistant keepers until the light was decommissioned in 1933. Some of the lighthouse

Crabtree Ledge Lighthouse

keepers were Charles W. Thurston, Joseph M. Gray, Amaziah Small, Edward Small, Alton Triveau, Jerome H. Peasely, Chester Brinkworth, Leon Brinkworth, Captain Joseph Whitmore, Ora Jordan, and Vassar Lee Quimby.

The Fresnel lens was removed and today sits in the Coast Guard Museum at Cherry Point, New Jersey. The lighthouse was sold to the Noyes family of Washington D.C. for the sum of $115. They later sold the lighthouse in 1937 to Fritz Allis, who summered on Hancock Point. He spent his honeymoon at the lighthouse with his bride, Tiense Gummere. A storm stranded the honeymoon couple for several days. A year later, Mr. Allis and friends brought a reed organ to the lighthouse. The organ was removed before the lighthouse fell over in February of 1950. A cold snap and heavy ice flow from Taunton Bay with an outgoing tide brought the Crabtree Ledge Lighthouse to its watery grave. Wreckers removed parts of the old cast iron caissons to be used in the Korean War effort.

The Steamer *Sebenoa* and the Crabtree Lighthouse became entangled in history. The

Crabtree Ledge Lighthouse

Sebenoa was constructed in 1880 by the Eastern
Steamboat Company, of Bath, Maine, and was used

Steamship *Sebenoa*

Courtesy Bar Harbor Historical Society

in the Boothbay Harbor area. The steamer was
about 100 feet long and displaced 87 tons. It had
been fitted with steam machinery from the Neafie &
Levy Company of Philadelphia. In 1888, she was
refitted with a new style double furnace and
horizontal crank that was constructed at the Goss
Iron Works. The *Sebenoa* carried freight and would
handle comfortably seventy five passengers. In
January of 1884, it was sold to the Maine Central
Railroad to be used on the Mount Desert Ferry run.
In 1911, the *Sebenoa* was sold to the Vinalhaven &
Rockland Ferry Service. She was resold in 1920 to
the Bridgeport Towing Line Company of

Crabtree Ledge Lighthouse

Connecticut.

During her time on the Mount Desert Ferry run, the *Sebenoa* made a lot of memories for the tourist and citizens who traveled through Frenchman's Bay. She was noted for the thousands of passengers she carried between the Hancock and Bar Harbor, Mount Desert Ferry Terminals. Many dignitaries

Courtesy Hancock Historical Society

were known to have sailed on her decks. Some of the dignitaries were United States President Grover Cleveland, Vice President Levi P. Morton, Secretary of State James G. Blaine, and U.S. Supreme Court Justice Melville W. Fuller. Vice President Morton and Justice Fuller were summer residents of Sullivan Harbor.

Crabtree Ledge Lighthouse

In August of 1884, the *Sebenoa* nearly came apart. It was discovered that she had a broken crank pin with only ½ inch remaining in the socket. If it had come apart, disaster and death would have followed. A day earlier, U.S. Secretary of State Blaine had been next to the engineer during an excursion and had been standing over the broken pin.

The *Sebenoa* carried the mail and was used for icebreaking service for Frenchman's Bay during its duration as a ferry for the Maine Central Railroad. On a few rare occasions, the *Sebenoa* failed to clear a path through the ice for other ships to follow.

From 1884 until 1889, Captain Oliver was in the wheelhouse. He made a serious character mistake on October 28, 1889. Aboard the steamer that day were the delegates of the Woman's Christian Temperance Union. The Captain decided that he needed a spirituous drink. While in the wheel house, he hoisted a rum jug to his mouth to take a swig. The jug had a bow of white ribbon attached due to someone giving this to him as a gift. It didn't go over well with the ladies and a complaint was filed to his superiors.

Captain Edgar P. Dickson was hired to replace Captain Oliver for the *Sebenoa's* eight mile run. Captain Dickson was honored in the newspapers of the day. He was an accomplished mariner, was liked by all whom knew him, and was noted for his bravery. In one incident, on November 7, 1895, Captain Dickson was returning to Bar Harbor from Rockland. A terrible storm arose and he stood for eight hours at the wheel, fighting the sea. The *Sebenoa* was towing a scow to be used by the company for gathering freight. The waves were so high that it seemed a possibility that the scow would be projected into the stern of the *Sebenoa*. The hawser snapped and the scow was lost for a short time. Most captains would have returned to port without the scow; few would have battled like Captain Dickson to recover the scow.

On October 1, 1896, with Captain Dickson at the wheel, the feed pipe on the boiler blew out. A cloud of steam and fire rushed out of the boiler and scalded Fireman McAvey and Engineer Dodge. Hand pumps were set to work and the fire was taken under control. The passengers were deathly frightened, but under the command of Captain Dickson their fears were alleviated. Captain Parker, operating the steamer *Ruth* saw the steam and smoke and came to the rescue. The *Ruth* towed the *Sebenoa* to Bar Harbor for repairs.

On February 3, 1898, several newspapers reported that the *Sebenoa* had saved Sullivan. Most of Frenchman's Bay was frozen and the ocean water between Hancock and Sullivan was nearly a solid sheet of ice all the way from the head of three bays to beyond Bean Island way below the falls. This was a grave situation for no mail, supplies, or passengers could be transported. The *Sebenoa* had a copper-clad hull and was the only hope for breaking the ice. She was in dry dock but came in a hurry, even though she had just had a new boiler installed and had been freshly painted. She went to work clearing two channels so the ice could flow. It was times like this that the local people felt great pride in the *Sebenoa* and her crew. The summer people developed a great friendship with the crew and each summer they enjoyed seeing each other for

Crabtree Ledge Lighthouse

the season. On July 20, 1895, the purser for the *Sebenoa* was making change when a gust of wind blew a $20 bill into the air from a passenger's hand and it landed in the water. A deck hand, Ellis Bray, saw the bill flutter to the water. In a flash, he dove into the water and came up with the twenty in his teeth. The crowd cheered as he pulled himself up onto the wharf. He was given five dollars as a reward.

On November 19, 1898, the *Sebenoa* ran into the Crabtree Ledge Lighthouse. She was on her way from Bar Harbor to Hancock with two passengers at 8:10 a.m. The crew was preparing breakfast on the lower deck to be served for the oncoming passengers at 8:35 a.m. Captain Dickson was in the pilothouse and Emery Davis, a deckhand, was steering. He was not experienced at using the compass and did not follow normal protocol. The steamer typically headed north directly for the lighthouse and approximately 300 feet away it would turn the helm to starboard, making the *Sebenoa* pass with the lighthouse on her port side. Captain Dickson was busy looking at a map of the

Crabtree Ledge Lighthouse

Coastal Pilot and was not paying attention. Mr. Davis was fixated on watching the compass. Crabtree Ledge Lighthouse Keeper Captain Charles Chester was standing on the gallery of the lighthouse. He saw the steamer coming at full speed toward him. He assumed that the captain had a message or parcel for him, as this was common practice at the time. Captain Chester was speechless and could do nothing to warn the *Sebenoa*. The steamer struck the lighthouse on her starboard side with a massive glancing blow. The impact could have been worse if it had been a head-on collision. Captain Dickson quickly took the wheel and continued to power the steamer until the *Sebenoa* came to rest on the beach just above the town wharf. The bow of the *Sebenoa* was destroyed and water was filling the engine room. Six feet of water filled her hull. Mr. William Cooper, the master mechanic for the Maine Central Railroad Co., was sent to determine the amount of damage. The bow was crushed, the shaft was sprung, and the rudderpost, as well as some timbers and beams, were broken. After making temporary repairs, the tugboat *Ralph Ross* towed the *Sebenoa* to Rockland. It took a year for the repairs to be completed. Some newspapers claimed that the weather was stormy and foul, while other papers contended that it was clear and sunny. Another version of this story is there was a verbal argument taking place between Captain Dickson and Mr. Davis. Mr. Davis was a little headstrong and followed the captain's orders to stay on course to a fault. Whatever the actual cause of the accident may never be known, but Captain Dickson was given back command of the *Sebenoa* on January 18, 1899; the date she was put back into service.

In July of 1903, one of the most favorite runs for all of the passengers was the afternoon cruise. She would leave Bar Harbor at 3:10 p.m.; stop at the Mount Desert Ferry terminals in Sorrento, Sullivan Harbor, and Hancock; and would return to Bar Harbor by 5:55 p.m. On July 20, 1904, the *Sebenoa* broke her shaft on passage from Sullivan to Hancock, Mount Desert Ferry Terminals. Her sister ship the *Norumbega,* of the same line, towed her to port. There were no injuries to any of the

Crabtree Ledge Lighthouse

passengers or crew and little damage to the mechanical equipment. The Maine Central Railroad Company had made plans to build a steel steamer to replace the *Sebenoa* after the 1904 season, but she stayed in service until being sold in the year of 1911.

Diving on the Crabtree Ledge Lighthouse

In 1993, we heard about the old Crabtree Ledge Lighthouse. We could not wait to see what was left and if any of the evidence about its past could be found. We learned that the lighthouse had been lit by a Fresnel Lens. These lenses are worth a fortune to antique dealers. We did not know at the time whether or not the lens was in the lighthouse when it fell over. Also, we heard of a reed organ that had once been taken out to the lighthouse. We knew that ivory keys could be worth a lot of money.

Crabtree Ledge Lighthouse

Once again, as Marlene would say, John was hoping to get rich quick. John was hoping to either get rich quick or to get rich in local history.

John knew because of its location it would be wise to take a veteran diver. He asked Eric Doak, a college buddy and excellent diver, if he would be willing to go on the adventure. Eric has always been a daredevil and has lived his life on the edge. He agreed wholeheartedly to be John's dive partner. Not wanting to leave the lobster boat unattended, John asked Marlene's brother-in-law, Robert "Robbie" Reed to tend the boat for them. He said he would be willing to man the boat with his 16 year old son, Chad.

John had no idea what they would see or what was left of the lighthouse. John decided that by looking at the charts, it would be best to dive at low tide on the incoming tide. This would increase the bottom time and help increase the visibility since clearer water would be coming in from offshore. They anchored the boat next to the ledge and rolled off with a net bag, wreck reel, surface buoy, and their down line. Beyond the normal dive gear, John carried a dive light to investigate the dark crevices created by the wreckage. Eric and John planned the dive and then would dive the plan. If they got separated, they were to search for each other for one minute and then surface. They decided, if there was an opening into the old lighthouse, they would only enter if it did not require them to take off their tanks to squeeze through the hole. This seemed like a safe plan. They circled the remains of the old caisson. In the 1950's, some salvage had taken place, but a great deal of old twisted debris was still present. They circled the ledge and could see a lot of bricks and slabs of concrete sitting on top of the ledge. On the western side of the ledge, there was an opening in the old caisson about three feet by three feet. John tied the line of his wreck reel to an old handle on the outside of the opening, entered into the remains, and noticed that the ceiling was circular. He had a hard time understanding what he was seeing inside the caisson. It was lying on its side and crushed in the middle like a soda can that had been stepped on creating a horseshoe appearance. The caisson appeared to go into the ledge and was below a lot of the old bricks and cement. John had no more than entered and turned on his flashlight when he became alarmed. On the inside of the structure, on the round walls, which was now the ceiling, the caisson was covered with sea anemones. Eric had followed him into the opening. Their bubbles were striking the rounded ceiling making a large air bubble. As the air bubbles struck this area of the caisson, it created a percolation effect, which caused the rust to drop from the overhead wall. This dark cloud made their visibility nearly zero. By positioning their faces closer to the bottom, they could see below the layer of rust. The rust continued on its downward progression as they continued to exhale into the water. John made a motion to Eric to get the heck out. Just as they were headed for the opening, John's light flooded and went out. John continued to follow Eric into the open water. Overhead obstructions are dangerous and should never be attempted without proper training and redundant gear. Such as two flashlights!

Crabtree Ledge Lighthouse

They made their way up to the surface and changed tanks for a second dive. During their surface interval, they informed Robbie and Chad of the close call. They agreed they would not be entering that caisson section again. Most of the next dive was in the 25 foot depth area. By looking at the charts, they planned to make their way down a little deeper and then circle the ledge while doing an investigation of the area. Shortly into their second dive, they located an enormous chain, which seemed to go through the debris field and out into about 30 feet of water. They followed it for about 80 feet and found many old porcelain cups and dishes. Most had chips and cracks but some were whole. They also found clay smoking pipes and old bottles. John figured that the lighthouse keepers had used the Atlantic Ocean as their dumping ground. Near the base of the lighthouse in about 20 feet of water, Eric and John located a four foot long piece of heavy brass with a piece of iron passing through it. They had no idea what it was. They tied a line to it and had Robbie pull it aboard the boat. To this day, John and Marlene really do not know what it is. The reed organ and the Fresnel Lens were what they were hoping to locate. Later through research, John discovered that these items had been removed years earlier before the lighthouse fell over.

In 1997, John took a job teaching marine trades at Narraguagus High School in Harrington, Maine. He brought the piece of brass they had recovered to the high school. Some nights, he was in charge of detention hall. He would offer the students an opportunity to have their detention cut in half, if they would assist in cleaning and buffing the brass object. All they had to do was spend 30 minutes sanding and cleaning the object and their hour detention would be considered served. This motivated the students to do a great job cleaning and putting a shine on it. Later, John and Marlene started giving lectures about diving in the local area to many historical societies. The object weighed close to 80 pounds and was too heavy to continually transport to lectures. We have since loaned it to the Hancock Historical Society, for this is the proper place to display this artifact.

Crabtree Ledge Lighthouse

In 1996, we became scuba instructors and later in the year we advanced our certifications to Master Scuba Diver Trainer (MSDT). As MSDTs, we are able to teach specialty dive classes; one being Underwater Archaeology Specialty Course. To become Underwater Archaeology Specialty Instructors, we wrote and design a program that had to be approved by the Professional Association of Diving Instructors (PADI).

In 2011, we were conducting an Underwater Archeology summer field school at the University of Maine at Machias. The field school's prerequisites required participants to be certified divers and to have taken our Underwater Archaeology class and pool lab. In July, we decided to take the students out to the lighthouse. We boarded our 20 foot *Corson* dive boat with a fellow PADI Assistant Instructor, Harry Fish Jr. from Jonesport, Maine. He brought his boat, the *Sundance,* to assist with transporting students and provided added safety during the dives. Harry would be the captain during the dives. We would supervise the divers. We tied the boats together and

Crabtree Ledge Lighthouse

left Philip Stroup on board to provide assistance to the divers. After assigning buddies, we determined each pair's destination and provide instructions on depths and times to be followed during the dives. We limited the depth to 50 feet and reinforced, if the buddies were separated, to search for one minute. If the buddies were not located, they were to surface and reunite. PADI Divemaster, Aaron Herzog and PADI Advanced Diver Kevin VanGorden were buddies. PADI Divemaster in Training Scott Bickford and PADI Advanced Diver Keith VanGorden were buddies. The Divemaster and Divemaster in Training were to lead their partners to predesignated and assigned areas.

We knew that years earlier a previous Underwater Archeology Student, Frank Salonic, of Pembroke, Maine, had found a copper deck iron near the Crabtree Ledge Lighthouse. We descended to about 35 feet in the same area where Frank had found the deck iron and within a few minutes Marlene found a copper smokestack. We could not believe our luck. We tied a line to the smokestack and released an orange signal buoy. The students

Crabtree Ledge Lighthouse

all noticed the marker buoy. When we surfaced, everyone was asking what we had found. John told them to guess. Scott Bickford said, "Knowing you, it probably is the lighthouse shitter." We all broke into laughter and John told Scott that he was not even close. Scott grabbed the orange marker buoy and pulled it up. To everyone's amazement, we had found a smokestack near the Crabtree Ledge Lighthouse. Along with the smokestack, we found large coffee mugs, which we believe had been sitting on the tables of the *Sebenoa* as the crew prepared for breakfast when it struck the lighthouse and sent items flying into the ocean. We gathered some broken pieces of porcelain dishware and some clay smoking pipes. When we arrived back at The Galley Restaurant, we matched the holes in the copper smokestack to the holes in the copper deck iron and they matched perfectly. We had originally thought this was off the *Sebenoa*, but research indicates the dimensions would not match. We believe this may be the smokestack and deck iron from the top section of the Crabtree Ledge Lighthouse.

103

Schooner Mabel E. Goss

The Schooner *Mabel E. Goss* was originally known as the British schooner *Lizzie B.* She was built in Port Grenville, Nova Scotia in 1890, having a gross tonnage of 95 tons and a net tonnage of 83 tons. She was two masted with a square stern and a decorative billet head. The *Lizzie B.* primarily was used as a lumber schooner and delivered boards to Boston from the Port Grenville area. Captain W.A. Howard was at the helm on her early voyages.

On October 12, 1894, the *Lizzie B.* was in route to Portland, Maine from Parrsboro, Nova Scotia, with Captain Belyea at the helm. She was carrying $500 worth of coal. A strong gust of wind broke off her foremast, but she was able to limp her way to Portland. She required $2,500 worth of repairs,

Schooner Mabel E. Goss

which equaled her total value.

Captain Howard was mastering the schooner on May 25, 1895, as she was carrying a load of lumber valued at $1000. The *Lizzie B.* was sailing from Two Rivers, Nova Scotia headed for Gloucester, Massachusetts. She wrecked on Libby Island Bar, Maine. Personnel from the life-saving station on Cross Island, six miles away, were able to save the crew of four, but only a small portion of her cargo. Before the wreck, the *Lizzie B.* was valued at $5,000 and afterwards at $2,900.

Since the schooner had wrecked in American waters, the *Lizzie B.* was taken to Machias, Maine, to be auctioned. She was purchased from the insurance company by Charles Robinson, Aaron Grant, George Waide and Samuel L. Bulson. The four owners were able to registered the schooner as an American Vessel. They constructed a "boot heel" poop deck on the hull of the schooner, which was their original design. In the year 1896, she was sold to John L. Goss and his family of Stonington, Maine, to be used for shipping granite. They listed Charles Robinson as the captain.

Schooner Mabel E. Goss

Drawing of Diver Harry Fish at the Helm of the Mabel E. Goss
"Boot Heel" Poop Deck

Drawing Courtesy of Michael Aruda

The Goss Family owned granite businesses and stone quarries. In 1887, the Goss family had acquired some property on Crotch Island, located off Stonington, Maine. They started a quarrying business and purchased the F.S. Warren quarry on the same Island in 1896. In the 1890's, they acquired a quarry on Moose Island. The family advertised their pink granite in newspapers across

Schooner Mabel E. Goss

the United States. The granite was used in some famous construction projects such as the U.S. Post Office Building in Lowell, Massachusetts; a dry-dock at Portsmouth, New Hampshire; the Pilgrim Monument at Provincetown, Massachusetts; and the Cape Cod Canal, Massachusetts.

The granite business entered a steep decline with the development of reinforced concrete. The Goss Family's last big contract was received in 1918 from the U.S. Government to expand a dry dock at East Boston. Most of the stone was carried by their two schooners the *Mary F. Lynch* and the *Mabel E. Goss*. Both had been specially rigged for the business of carrying stone. After the completion of the East Boston dry dock, only rough stone was shipped. In 1922, the Goss family sold Moose Island, but continued quarrying on Crotch Island until the end of World War II. In 1965, the quarry was reopened to take out stone for the John F. Kennedy Memorial at Arlington Cemetery. Today, the quarries are operated on a limited basis for the manufacturing of decorative items by the New England Stone Company.

Schooner Mabel E. Goss

The *Mabel Goss* was also used for other jobs such as carrying general cargo on return trips after delivering stone. Captain Paschell was her master on most of her voyages. She had been rigged with a steam engine on the deck for the lifting of heavy stone. When she was later hired out as a wrecker, the steam engine was perfect for assisting with gathering salvage material.

Schooner Mabel E. Goss
Circa 1905

Courtesy Sullivan Sorrento Historical Society

One of her jobs was the salvage of the schooner *Annie E. Rudolph*. The *Rudolph* had an early

Schooner Mabel E. Goss

morning collision on May 9th of 1897, with the iron tug *Paoll*. The *Rudolph* sank off from Nauset, Cape Cod, Massachuessets. In August of 1897, the Goss was salvaging the cargo of pipe from the wreck. Captain Paschal had diver Lincoln Russell working 60 feet below the surface inside the *Rudolph*. The three crew members bodies had not been recovered at this point. The crew members were Captain Gardner, First Mate Snell and a seaman. The diver was shocked to find two human skulls. One was inside the vessel the other was on the deck. The diver was convinced he had found Captain Gardiner's head. He assumed that the body of the Captain was under the cabin deck. He reasoned since the stern of the vessel was cut off, the action of the water would force the body under the deck. The other skull was assumed to be that of a sailor. Diver Russell, also, saw another whole body on the deck tangled in wreckage. He decided not to try and recover right then but would at a later time. Sadly, he was never able to find this body again. The two skulls were placed in a bucket of salt water and were later dried. The *Goss* sailed into Potter A

Schooner Mabel E. Goss

Wrightington's Wharf with the skulls on the deck. A crowd gathered and was aghast at the gruesome scene. What was particularly upsetting was that in the crowd were the relatives of Captain Gardner!

The Schooner *Mabel E. Goss* had additional captains during her maritime career. Captain Coombs, Captain Duke, and Captain Fraser were all employees who were contracted by the Goss family to master the vessel. On June 6, 1911, the *Goss* was employed to do a wrecking job on the Schooner *Teresa D. Baker*, which had wrecked on the south shore, off from the town of Duxbury, Massachusetts. The hull of *Baker* was a complete loss. The *Goss* was able to retrieve spars, rigging, and fittings.

The *Goss's* crew came to the realization they could earn a lot of money in this type of work. The financial holdback in a business venture of this type was waiting for the next wreck. In July of 1911, she started a third career as a treasure salvager. The owners decided to stay in northern waters to try and recover copper, gold, and silver payrolls from sunken schooners. They started their first venture

Schooner Mabel E. Goss

in Vineyard Sound, between Woods Hole and Martha's Vineyard.

The Schooner *Goss* had her troubles, but the crews were usually able to overcome them. On June 21, 1914, the *Goss* slammed into a ledge known as Logy Ledge. It was near the Wood Island Life Saving Station, off Kittery, Maine. The crew from the station responded at once. Since the tide was coming, she was able to clear herself off the ledge.

The amount of stone to be shipped went down considerably during the 1920's. The *Goss* still found work in Sullivan, Maine, to carry quarry stone for some of the active granite quarries. She typically loaded stone in Sullivan, Maine, and made a trip to the Boston area to unload. On her return trip, she would carry a load of general merchandise to make the voyage profitable.

On May 9th, 1921, the *Goss* was on her way up into Taunton Bay over the Sullivan Falls, when the wind and tide forced her onto the center ledge. She could not be freed. The crew of three planned to return the next day and try a second time to free her.

Schooner Mabel E. Goss

Captain Fraser secured their belongings inside the cabin and put a lock on the hasp of the cabin door. That night there was a larger tide than the one during the day. The *Mabel E. Goss* floated off from the center ledge, came up through the falls and struck the first set of ledges on the Sullivan side of Taunton Bay. The keel was forced against the ledge and the *Goss* rolled onto its side. The combined weight of the two masts and mounted steam engine were too much for the schooner to stay upright with the force from the incoming tide. She sank in an eddy on the east side of the ledge in about an average depth of ten feet.

Poignantly, she went from being a wrecker to being salvaged by the local citizens. The citizens would gather her valuable remains predominantly at low tide. Sadly, the only treasure she may have carried was bootleg alcohol. This was a common contraband during the prohibition era. Now the tables had turned, the old wrecker had become a wreck herself.

Schooner Mabel E. Goss

Diving on the Mabel E. Goss

In February 1980, John was talking to his grandfather, Lester Mosley. John told him he wanted to search for treasure and asked if he knew of a shipwreck that might provide treasure. John needed to write a report for a history class he was taking at the University of Maine at Machias. His grandfather suggested that he dive the *Mabel E. Goss*. His grandfather informed him that he was friends with some of the Butler brothers from Hancock, who had salvaged material from the wreck years earlier. He provided John with a location where he thought the wreck might be. This venture would have the makings of a great history paper and would provide John with an exciting activity he would be able to use for improving his grade. John felt fortunate to have George Thurston as one of his UMM History Professors. Mr. Thurston was familiar with the area and gave his approval for John to document this experience for credit towards the class.

Schooner Mabel E. Goss

John recruited his cousin, Eric White, to help him. John borrowed a 12 foot aluminum rowboat from his uncle, James White. Eric and John launched the rowboat at the old landing on the Sullivan side of the bridge. John loaded his dive gear and brought rope to help recover anything of interest. They could not find any oars for the boat. The closest paddles they could find were two snow shovels. They were quite a sight rowing with snow shovels, but it worked fairly well. They headed out about 40 minutes before low tide. The current assisted with carrying them down to the ledge where the wreck was supposedly located.

With about eight feet of water under the boat, John rolled out, dived down and scoured the ledge. The water was biting cold. There was great visibility, which is uncommon for this area. What assisted with the visibility that winter was the ice had covered the mud flats in the upper bays and prevented silt from moving with the currents. Also, Egypt, Taunton and Hog Bays have large amounts of filter feeders such as clams, mussels and scallops that remove plankton. John estimated there was close to 30 feet of visibility. The current had slowed, and Eric was able to maneuver the rowboat close to John's bubbles. After being down for about ten minutes, John came across the frame and pistons of a steam engine in about six feet of water. John knew that the *Goss* had been carrying an engine on the deck. To the north of the engine, about 30 feet away, he found ship timbers. He had found the remains of the *Goss*!

John swam around and looked for artifacts that he could take back to use in his college presentation. He was between the steam engine and the timbers when he saw two large brass joints. They were attached by a four foot heavy piece of two inch thick iron. There was a wooden spoke wheel on the end. John had no idea what this object was. He decided that he would dig a hole underneath it and try to dislodge it. He could not budge it. He had Eric bring the boat above the artifact. John placed a ½ inch nylon line over the center of the boat and tied it to the artifact. His plan was to use the boat to lift the object as the tide rose. He tightened the line, and as the tide began to rise, to his amazement, the object did not budge. The freeboard of the boat was shrinking! Eric was concerned that the boat was going to sink. He advised John to untie the line. John went down and tried to untie the rope, but could not loosen the knot. He knew the worst thing that could happen was he would have to use his leg knife to cut the rope. John decided to try a Z-drag by going to the middle of the lift line and pulling as hard as he could. He started pulling in the middle of the line and the object finally broke loose. John had Eric pull the object up. It was too heavy for them to lift it into the boat. They tied it to the stern of the boat and let it dangle. Due to the weight of the object hanging off the boat, John did not dare to board the boat for fear there would be another wreck. The incoming tide was rapidly filling the bays. They were headed towards the landing with Eric using the snow shovels and John holding onto a line attached to the boat. Eric was trying to steer the boat towards shore; they were being swept under the bridge. While holding onto the line attached to the boat, John was able to descend and make his way along

Schooner Mabel E. Goss

the bottom to the shoreline. Once on the shore, John was able to pull the boat to the landing.

The item must have had something to do with the lifting apparatus on the steam engine. Years later while employed as a math/science teacher at Machias Memorial High School, John was able to cut away the iron and have students sand blast the two brass joints. He engraved the top of the brass joints with facts about the *Mabel E. Goss.*

In the summer of 2002, John was diving on the wreck of the *Mabel E. Goss* and his father, Gerald Daley, stayed aboard John's lobster boat to tend John's dive. They were able to remove a brass steam valve from the steam engine. They engraved their names and date on it. They later donated the artifact to the Sullivan Sorrento Historical Society.

In 2003, Marlene and John were teaching PADI scuba classes at the University of Maine at Machias. After becoming certified to teach Underwater Archaeology, we joined an organization from Maryland known as Maritime Archaeological Historical Society, MAHS. We decided to follow their protocol and to run an Underwater

Schooner Mabel E. Goss

Archaeology Summer Field School through the University of Maine at Machias, UMM. During the spring semester, we taught the prerequisite course Underwater Archaeology, class and pool lab. This allowed those students to be eligible for the seven-day field school offered during the summer.

On April 28, 1988, President Reagan signed into law the Abandoned Shipwreck Act (ASA). The purpose of the ASA is to give a title to certain abandoned shipwrecks that are located in state waters to the respective states and to clarify that the states have management authority over those abandoned shipwrecks. The law has had its critics because of how ambiguously it has been written. Many salvagers claim that the U.S. Government should be required to explain why a wreck is historical and why it needs protection. The law doesn't apply to military ships or to shipwrecks that lie on Native American Land.

We needed approval from the Maine State Museum in Augusta to run an underwater archaeology survey on the *Mabel E. Goss*. They granted permission to do a survey and to preserve selected items. They wanted to make sure that the items would be placed in a location on display for the public to view. We decided to only take items that could be easily preserved.

During the winter of 2002-2003, we started recruiting students for this educational program. We were familiar with a wonderful group of college students that had shown an interest in participating in an Underwater Archeology Field School. We chose students by their strengths that would enhance our weaknesses. We were not real familiar with the construction of schooners. We had both completed the MAHS coursework but we did not feel comfortable identifying structural parts of the *Mabel E. Goss*. We felt we needed experienced divers to assist students during the challenging dives within the strong currents of Taunton Bay. Two people we knew that would be assets in these areas were Harry Fish and Frank Salonick. Harry had built sailing vessels and had been a diver for many years. He had logged numerous dives since 1963; he had taken some of our other classes; and was working towards becoming a Divemaster.

Schooner Mabel E. Goss

Frank has been a professional diver for over twenty years, has countless hours diving in salmon cages, has experience diving in low visibility with strong currents; and has taken other courses from us. We felt the two of them had great knowledge of and experience in diving as well as had been great leaders within our other classes. They would be able not only to take direction but would be able to provide the leadership needed to assist with making the class a successful adventure. Adding these two divers would be beneficial to us as well as to the students. Their knowledge would assist with reaching our goal of obtaining an underwater survey of the schooner *Mabel E. Goss*. The dive students, Jessica Wagner, Michael Arruda, and Melissa Rudin, were Marine Biology majors attending the University of Maine at Machias and could identify the marine life in the area. Jessie Daley, our daughter, was a high school student at Sumner Memorial High School and was very familiar with the local history. Aaron Gilpatrick was our volunteer photographer, who had experience taking not only regular photographs but underwater pictures as well.

When setting up a project like this the number one priority is safety. A safety diver must be certified with a rating of Rescue Diver or higher and the Rescue Diver must be identified before each dive. The Rescue Diver's responsibilities are to have their equipment ready to assist in an emergency, monitor all divers' water time, record surface intervals, and to document starting and ending air pressures for each diver. The Rescue Diver should be located in a high position on the dive boat. They should keep a close watch on the divers' bubbles or their marker buoys.

The divers were paired and had agreed to follow safe diving standard procedures. Such as, if you became separated from your partner, you would search underwater for one minute, surface, reunite, and descend. The students were able to stay with their partners most of the time but sometimes current and low visibility caused separation. We tried to dive within one hour before and one hour after high slack, allowing us to anchor the boats near the wreck and the visibility to stay as clear as possible. The current was not as much as a problem near slack tide, but when it started running it could be unbearable. We were able to complete multiple dives during this two hour period because on an average, the depths of the dives were in 16 feet of water. We really did not have to worry about nitrogen buildup due to being at such shallow depths. The PADI dive planner states that as long as you do not go below 35 feet, your water time will not require a decompression stop before surfacing. Divers were constantly monitoring their time, because time appears to pass by more quickly while you are busy. The students were always amazed at the length of their time spent underwater and stated even though they knew how long the dives were, the dives seemed to be much shorter than they really were.

The UMM Underwater Archaeology Field School Class conducted the survey for the purposes of assessing the site for its archeological value and to determine its viability for future research. The class documented the procedures used and Melissa and Jessie compiled and recorded the events in the

Schooner Mabel E. Goss

form of a daily diary. The class documented a list of present marine life living on the wreck to determine the environmental impact of the Mabel E. Goss. Michael and Jessica created a visual list and description of the identified marine life.

On the first day of the survey, Michael and Harry set a baseline through the middle of the wreckage. They hammered two three foot steel bars into the bottom with a seven-pound splitting maul. Due to the strenuous nature and difficulty of the task, John entered the water to assist with setting the baseline datum points. It is very difficult in water to swing and hit an object due to things appearing to be 33 percent larger and closer. As well as when the maul would hit the bar, the diver would rise from the bottom due to Newton's Third Law of Motion. While John was swinging the maul, Harry applied added weight to John to assist with keeping him on the bottom and allowing more force from the maul as it struck the bar. Needless to say, this looked like a scene from a Three Stooges Movie. On the datum points, a steel cable was connected. To make it taut, we previously added a turnbuckle on both ends of the cable. A 100 foot tape measure was stretched and attached along the cable in order for the students to complete the trilateration of the objects found. This baseline was used in developing the site-diagram due to having two of the trilateration points used when locating the placement of objects. Trilateration is the process used in obtaining the location of an object by using the object as the third datum point. The three datum points were plotted on graph paper and a site diagram was created indicating where the objects were in relation to the baseline.

On the second day of diving, the students were involved in site preparation such as removal of kelp and checking for anything that may be hazardous to the students such as broken glass or sharp objects.

On the third day, the students placed red numbered flags next to any artifacts or pieces of wreckage of distinction and trilateration was completed.

On the fourth day, the divers photographed or drew pictures of the red flagged objects.

On the fifth day, a ferrous and non-ferrous

metals survey of the wreck was recorded.

On the sixth and seventh day, the metal study was completed by digging four test pits where hits were made by the metal detector. These test pits were used to determine what the metal object was and to help with an accurate measurement of strata. These areas would also determine how deep the wreckage was buried. The timbers from the wreck were discovered as deep as four and half feet below the gravel bottom of the bay. The artifacts that were taken and preserved for the Sullivan Sorrento Historical Society are as follows: two ships knees, a lead deck drain, an 1858 Mason jar and lid, a granite block, and a wooden barrel top.

We were hoping to locate and remove a brass identification plaque that would be located on the top of the steam engine. The problems in recovering this object were due to the engine landing upside down at the time of sinking, weighing about a ton, and had been partially buried in gravel over the years. We needed to flip the engine over to gain access to the top of the engine and hopefully locate the plaque. We had decided for safety reasons to have only two divers in the water when trying to upright the steam engine. Harry and Frank were chosen to place a lift bag on one side of the engine. The plan was to lift one side of the motor which would allow the two of them to push it over. We decided to design a lifting device using a skidder inner tube because when fully inflated the tube would have a lifting force of about 3400 pounds. We designed a lifting device by using an eight inch PVC pipe elbow, folding the skidder inner tube in half and passing it through the pipe with equal portions of the tube exposed on both ends of the elbow. We made sure the stem was on the outside portion of the tube in the mid-section of the exposed area on one side of the elbow for easy access. The elbow was attached to the engine by a white 3/4 inch nylon ropes and then the tube was inflated. Harry and Frank inflated the tube until it became so disfigured. It stretched all the way to the surface. Since the tube had reached the surface, its lifting capacity had ended. We feared that it would explode and cause a shock wave! This could cause Frank and Harry to have ruptured eardrums. Harry removed the valve stem spring so the tire would slowly deflate. The air remained in the tube due to it being so disfigured it had pinched off the air access back to the valve stem. Harry cut the attached rope between the steam engine and the skidder tube. He felt a noticeable shock wave as the tube went flying to the surface. This was a great learning experience for all involve even though we were not able to roll the engine and recover the plaque. MAHS published our underwater archeology survey in their 2004 Spring News Quarterly.

In July of 2009, Jessie Daley, Megan McGonagle, and John Murphy were diving on the *Goss*. Jessie had dived on the wreck numerous times since being a student during the 2003 Summer Field School. They dove from our 20 foot Corson pleasure boat anchored above the wreck. Jessie became aware of a disturbance amongst the beams, which was most likely caused by ice. During the spring thaw, ice will drift down from the upper bays and may catch on parts of the wreckage and move those pieces as the tide drains. To Jessie's astonishment, she noticed within the wreckage the cabin door from the poop deck which had not been visible on previous dives. She signaled Megan and John to assist her in removing it from the wreckage. Due to the increase in the current flow, they were not able to bring the object to the boat. They left it on the bottom sliding it under some beams to keep it from drifting away. Upon their return, Jessie informed us of her find.

The next day while diving from our lobster boat, Jessie and John (Daley) were able to retrieve the door with the assistance of the pot hauler. We then used a preservation method of submerging the door for two years in fresh water then covering the door with a solution of polyethylene glycol, PEG.

In August of 2014, Marlene and John were teaching an Advanced Open Water Class. We decided as part of the five required dives to include a boat dive and a wreck dive. The students were Brad Kennedy, Tyler Norton, and Jeff Leighton. Earlier in the day, John had placed an anchor next to the *Goss's* steam engine. He tied our 31 foot Duffy, *Marlene & 3Aces*, to the anchor line. We

Schooner Mabel E. Goss

had Marlene and Tyler, and Brad and Jeff as partners for the dives. Tyler and Marlene were the first to go down the anchor line to make sure the anchor was set. After securing the anchor, the other two divers would join them and they would explore the area around the wreck for 20 minutes, surface and declared the boat dive over. There was a light incoming current with about nine feet of visibility.

The second dive was the wreck dive and involved studying the remains of the *Goss*. The dive partners would return to the wreckage using the anchor line as a down line and follow the same dive plan as used during the previous dive. When Brad and Jeff landed at the base of the engine, Brad started his search and saw a three inch brass Eagle Lock lying on the bottom with the shackle still locked but bent. At one time, the lock had been obviously under a large amount of stress due to it needing a great amount of force to bend the thick shackle. This most likely is the lock Captain Fraser used on the *Mabel E. Goss's* cabin door the day he left the wreck on the center ledge of the Sullivan Falls.

Schooner Mabel E. Goss

Patent 1914 Eagle Six Lever Brass Padlock
(Recovered by PADI Diver Brad Kennedy)

Daley Collection

Schooner Abbie Bursley

The schooner *Abbie Bursley* was constructed in Camden, Maine in 1864. The owner and first Captain was David N. Kelly of Centerville, Massachusetts. In the American Lloyd's Register, she is listed as being 309 tons, 119 feet long, 29 feet breadth, 9 feet depth and a 12 foot draft. She was constructed of mixed materials of oak and pine, with copper and iron fasteners. Her first homeport was Boston, Massachusetts. Today, her final resting spot is on the bottom of Taunton Bay in Sullivan, Maine.

Schooners were used to assist the Union Army during the Civil War and were in high demand. The captains and their crews earned money based on the size of their vessel. In 1861, Captain David N. Kelley had been the captain of the bark *Island City* from Boston's Fort Warren carrying confederate prisoners to Fortress Monroe in Virginia. Since Captain Kelley was involved in the government charter business, he was able to easily secure another contract. In November 1864, as soon as the *Abbie Bursley* was completed, Captain Kelley was able to obtain a government contract to carry captured confederate munitions from the James River in Virginia back to the Washington

Schooner Abbie Bursley

D.C. arsenal. In her first year of sailing, she was put into service as a chartered schooner for the Union Army. The *Abbie Bursley* was paid every month based on her tonnage. A standard payment of $4.00 per ton would have earned the *Abbie Bursley's* captain and crew members a total payment of $1,236 per month which was a considerable amount of money for that time period.

In the years following the war, the *Abbie Bursley* was involved in standard shipping along the east coast of the United States, as well as along the South American coast. Cargoes she carried were guano from the Caribbean, coal from Philadelphia, and lumber and ice from New England. Later in her life, she was reinforced to carry heavy loads of granite from Maine.

The *Abbie Bursley* had numerous owners, captains, and crews. From 1864 to 1869, she was the property of Captain David N. Kelley. By spring of 1869, the *Bursley* had been sold to D. W. Bearse. Many voyages of the *Bursley* nearly ended in complete disaster. Shipping was a difficult business with few navigational aids, poor charts, limited markers, fog, and bad weather. On May 26, 1869, Captain James Henry

Schooner Abbie Bursley

Parker, a well-known captain from Osterville, Massachusetts, was put in charge of the *Bursley*. He was a member of the Freemasons, Republican Party, and a churchgoer. The father of two children, his life had not been easy. He had previously lost two other children as infants. His first wife, Velina Lovell Parker, succumbed to illness in 1862.

The *Abbie Bursley* was sailing from Cape Cod to Philadelphia with a load of coal when a storm unleased its furry at the end of Long Island near Montauk Point. The sea became violent and, without warning, the boom swung across the deck and knocked a crewman and the 39 year old captain overboard. The crew was able to save the seaman, but could not help the captain, who was lost at sea. His body was never recovered. Sadly, his second wife, Louisa, was on board and witnessed the tragedy. First Mate Charles E. Bearse was given the command of the schooner, but bad luck was to follow them on their return trip. They struck a ledge in almost the exact same spot where Captain Parker had lost his life a little over a month earlier. The crew had to jettison 100 tons of coal to lighten her load so she could be towed off the ledge by a steamer. The *Bursley* was

Schooner Abbie Bursley

taken to a shipyard in Newport, Rhode Island and later taken to Gardner, Maine, to be rebuilt. In the same year in the same location, Montauk Point, the grim reaper seemed not only to be after the *Abbie Bursley* but after the Parker family as a whole. James's brother, Captain Frank C. Parker and his son, David, while on the schooner *Mary Milenes,* were lost when their ship was wrecked.

For most of the year of 1870, the *Bursley* was out of commission, but was sold to C. A. Lovell & Son, who put her back into the trade with Captain O. P. Bearse and Captain James Baker handling most of the helm duties through 1873. Lovell and his son were the sole owners, unlike in previous years where other owners had a majority of the shares in the *Bursley.* Captain James Baker was a consignee for the *Abbie Bursley* for the years 1871, 1876, 1877, and 1878.

On May 14, 1872, the *Abbie Bursley* was carrying 230,215 board feet load of lumber from a New York port to Georgetown, D.C. There were high seas and the *Abbie Bursley* lost her load of lumber, jibboom, rudder and two seamen. The schooner *Joseph Baymore* of Darien, Georgia, was underway off the coast of Cape

Schooner Abbie Bursley

Hatteras, North Carolina, on the 18th of May. Abraham C. Jones of Hyannis, Massachusetts, and another seaman both of the schooner *Abbie Bursley* came into view as they were floundering in the ocean. The *Baymore* recovered the two seamen. The *Abbie Bursely* was towed to Lewes, Delaware, by the steamer *Tonawanda*. The *Abbie Bursley* received her repairs and continued within the shipping trade. The following samplings from the year of 1876 show some of the trade the *Bursley* ventured in during her sailing days. She not only sailed in the United States but was chartered for trips to other countries. On May 10th, 1876, the receipt shows where the *Bursley* paid $233.28 to cover items purchased and fees to C. Lovell & Son for a chartered trip to Trinidad and back for which they would receive $2,223.00. Trips below the equator were very common for vessels of her size.

1876 Receipt

Courtesy William Brewster Nickerson Cape Cod History Archives

On July 21st, 1876, the *Abbie Bursley* purchased the

135

Schooner Abbie Bursley

right to ship 471 tons of coal from the A. G. Fisher Co. The Fisher Co. charged a brokerage fee of six cents per ton of coal for a total of $28.26 to the *Bursley*. The A. G. Fisher Co. was located in Philadelphia, Pennsylvania. To complete the purchase of the 471

1876 Receipt

Courtesy William Brewster Nickerson Cape Cod History Archives

tons of coal, the *Bursley* would pay $4.00 per ton for the coal including loading at the wharf for a total of $1,884.00.

On September 28th, 1876, the *Bursley* purchased the rights from the Fitz Brothers & Co. for a 446 ton load. On October 30, she paid 30 cents per ton for a total of $133.80 for the load and a five percent commission of $6.69 to the Fitz Brothers. A brokerage fee was

1876 Receipt

Courtesy William Brewster Nickerson Cape Cod History Archives charged by all of the companies who would secure the trade. Many of the brokerage firms owned the wharfs used for loading and unloading the cargos. This was a common pratice within the shipping trade by brokerage firms.

While on her trip, the *Bursley* had to be towed by steamboat *Nabby C. and Owners* from Kittingers to Stream for a fee of $4.00 on October 3rd, 1876. This was common practice to be towed in to the harbor to a company wharf to unload and load merchandise. The common towing price would range from $4.00-$8.00.

1876 Receipt

Courtesy William Brewster Nickerson Cape Cod History Archives

On February 3, 1880, the *Bursley* with Captain William B. Baker and a crew of seven found themselves in a terrible plight. The schooner had set its anchors during a severe storm about 150 yards from the breakwater at Lanesville, Massachusetts. The crew of Life Saving Station Number 2 saw the *Bursley* in its perilous predicament. They quickly went to work and were able to position a mortar apparatus on shore near the *Bursley*. The crewmen of the Life Saving Station soon discovered that local fishermen had rescued the *Bursley* crew. Captain Baker stayed at the station whereas all of his men were taken into town for shelter. During the night, the storm continued to rage, and the schooner dragged its anchors until it came ashore. The *Bursley* was carrying a load of ice and was headed for Philadelphia. The following day the crew was taken back to the *Bursley* and was able to remove their personal belongings. They were given free passes aboard the Eastern Railroad to Boston. The schooner was severely damaged and taken to a shipyard where numerous repairs were needed and completed. On December 7, 1885, once again bad luck, bad judgment, poor steering or all of the above struck the *Abbie Bursley*. She was headed for the port of Vineyard Haven, Massachusetts, when she struck the schooner *Lewis King*, of Ellsworth, Maine. The *King* was at her mooring. The collision ripped the jibboom and all of its attachments from the *King*, while the *Bursley* only lost a davit.

Captain William H. Parker was the captain aboard

Schooner Abbie Bursley

the ship for different durations of time between 1879 and 1882. His expertise in navigation was needed for particular voyages. He made regular trips to South

Captain William Parker   Captain James H. Parker

Courtesy William Brewster Nickerson Cape Cod History Archives

America and during the winter he was involved in the ice trade. He usually brought along his wife, Jennie Bearse Parker, their two children Horace and Louise, and sometimes his sister Hattie Parker. Other captains that were placed at the helm were Captain Allen in 1881 and Captain Hamilton from 1886 to 1888. Throughout the years, the *Abbie Bursley* called Boston, Osterville, or Barnstable, Massachusetts, her homeports.

In 1889, the schooner moved to Hancock, Maine. During that year, she was under the control of Captain A. Crabtree of Hancock. She was able to make her

Schooner Abbie Bursley

payload from granite. The *Burlsey* would ship granite from the Stone Quarry of Crabtree & Havey in Sullivan, Maine. Most of her voyages were to Boston, New York, and Philadelphia. On her return trips, a normal cargo would be coal and general merchandise to be sold at the quarry store owned by Havey. Ownership of the schooner went from Lovell & Son in 1891 to Crabtree & Havey. The stone company chose Captain Bickford to run the ship. He continued to be the captain until she met her final misfortune in 1895. The accident that transpired involved the ledge by the Gordon Cemetery on the Sullivan side of Taunton Bay. The bay has extremely powerful currents that can make it difficult for sailing vessels to operate, especially ones that do not have auxiliary motors to assist with propulsion or steering. According to Howard "Tomcat" Gordon, who was repeating a story told by his farther, the *Bursley* was headed up the bay to a stone wharf when she struck the sunker. This ledge is below the surface about one foot during low tide. The *Bursley* had a draft of 12 feet. Even at high tide, it would have been too dangerous to attempt to clear this ledge. The ledge goes nearly one-third of the way across Taunton

Schooner Abbie Bursley

Bay from Sullivan. Upon striking the ledge, her hull began taking on water due to the massive hole created by the impact. The incoming tide was so strong; it pushed the ship over the ledge. The hand pumps onboard kept her afloat for a while, as she was floundering trying to make the wharf. She was not able to make the wharf and sank near the shore. The men made it safely to the land. The ship was unable to be repaired. Tragically, she is resting about 500 yards up the bay from the ledge on the Sullivan side next to the Blaisdell Cemetery in about 15 feet of water. This location is directly across the bay from the Hancock Riverside Cemetery. Some may argue she finally found a peaceful resting place after having such a turbulent life.

Diving on the Schooner *Abbie Bursley*

In July of 1990, we were pulling lobster traps in Taunton Bay about 60 yards out from the beach in front of the Blaisdell Cemetery. One of the trap lines was entangled and would not budge. John discussed with fellow lobsterman Tomcat where his trap was entangled. At this time, Tomcat was a man in his 60's who had lobster fished in Taunton Bay nearly his entire life. He told John that most likely the trap was entangled within the remains of an old wreck within that area. John asked him if he knew the type of ship and what the name of it might be. Tomcat said it was on old schooner that carried stone called the *Abbie Bursley*. Tomcat's father, a lifetime lobstermen, had told him the story of the old vessel and her fate. John needed to recover his trap and thought it would be a great adventure to dive on the old wreck.

John prepared his scuba gear for the following day. Marlene and John have been avid divers and did not think that this dive would be very difficult. Marlene wanted to join him, but we were afraid to have our 20 foot Eastport lobster boat left alone over the wreck. The current in this area runs around seven knots during the ebb and flow of the tides. During slack high or low tide, there is an approximate 20 minutes time frame with very little tidal movement. If for some reason the boat broke loose from its anchored position and drifted in the current, it could be a long swim to the boat, especially if it ended up in the middle of the bay. Hence, Marlene stayed aboard the boat. John was initiating the dive at dead high slack to avoid being swept away. The depth of the dive was in about 20 feet of water. The visibility in Taunton Bay can vary greatly. On some days, there may be only inches of visibility but on a good day there can be about 20 feet. The concern would not be the clarity of the water, but the obstructed view caused by the kelp. Not being sure of what the warp line had become entangled with, John did know he would be landing in the colossal kelp bed that was visible at low tide. The kelp had to have attached itself to something of substance within that location due to the strength of the current in order for it to survive. He used the warp line as the down line and slid his left hand in front of him due to not knowing what was creating the entanglement or the exact depth. He carried with him a rope with a marker buoy and two knives and pulled himself down the warp line. As he continued down the line, he would part the kelp in order to proceed without losing his grasp on the down line. The long dragon tail kelp was constantly wrapping itself around his body. He cleared the kelp away from the entangled area once landing on the bottom. The warp line was too badly wrapped around an old beam to be untangled. Thus, John continued to follow the warp line to the trap he needed to recover.

Once reaching his trap, he cut the warp line from the trap bridle and attached the line he carried. John would then be able to recover his trap upon boarding the boat. Before starting the dive, John notified Marlene that after untangling the trap, he would be exploring the surroundings. Swimming slowly and pulling through the forest of kelp, he could see old ship beams going in . and out of the bottom of the bay. The bottom was mostly made up of sand, pin gravel, and old clamshells. He noticed there were three larger beams lying parallel with the shoreline. There were old iron and brass pins embedded in the beams. He could feel the current starting to intensify and did not want the current to become a problem while attempting to board the boat. John was excited to inform Marlene about his find. He knew that Tomcat had a good memory and that we had found the *Abbie Bursley*.

In the years to follow, we dived on the wreck

Schooner Abbie Bursley

numerous times to investigate any historical interests that may be at the site. On one of these occasions, a very strange thing took place. We were diving in the early summer of 1994 from our lobster boat. We had left Marlene's sister Marilyn and her husband Robbie Reed aboard the boat. We dropped anchor and it quickly caught itself in the wreck. The condition of the wreck as compared to the first dive seemed to be deteriorating. In a few hundred years, only remnants of the wreckage may exist. Only if the wood is buried or recovered and preserved, will there be any evidence of the ship. Wood bearing mollusk called terra cotta worms had eaten a large portion of the beams that were uncovered and most of the decking. Scallop drags had hit the wreck on numerous occasions causing damage. We were concerned with artifacts that could be saved and preserved to be put on display would be lost if not recovered.

Marlene was digging on the side of an old beam and John was on the other side about 15 feet away. We could clearly see each other through the kelp as it was wavering in the light current. John was looking at an old piece of corroded iron when all of a sudden something forced him to the bottom quickly with a great amount of impact and held him there for what appeared to be a minute. In reality, it was only a few seconds. Instantly, John thought that a lobsterman had thrown a trap off his boat and it had landed on his back. John rolled around quickly and could not see what had held him down and there was not a trap in sight. He was confused by the incident and looked for Marlene. She was still about 15 feet away and nothing seemed to be out of the ordinary. She was digging and had just found some black marbles that were probably from one of the previous captain's children. About ten minutes had gone by since John's incident, when Marlene appeared from over the backside of a beam. She swam over to him and shook her finger in his face like he had done something to her. He shrugged his shoulders. We headed for the anchor line and proceeded to the surface. Marlene pulled back her mask, took out her regulator, and exclaimed, "Thanks a lot for pushing me down on the bottom and holding me there!" John has been known to pull a gag now and then, so she assumed John had attempted one on her. John looked her in the eyes and told her it was not him and that the same thing had happened to him! She looked bewildered by his response. Marlene asked, "What was it?" John responded, "I have no idea!"

In 1996, we became Open Water Instructors through Professional Association of Diving Instructors, PADI. We taught private lessons for local students. With fellow PADI Open Water Instructor, Stan Smith of Jonesboro, Maine, we also taught PADI Open Water, Advanced Open Water, Rescue, and Divemaster certification courses at the University of Maine at Machias, UMM.

Further training and education advanced us from PADI Open Water Instructors to the PADI Master Scuba Diver Trainer, MSDT, level of certification. This allows us to offer different specialty certifications to our students depending on their diving experiences. We were approved by PADI to offer 12 different specialties due to our previous diving experiences, educational course work, and course development. There are prerequisites before you may take certain courses or specialties. All students must be Open Water certified to be able to move on to Advanced Open Water. The Advanced Open Water Class has a

Schooner Abbie Bursley

minimum of five different dives. A typical Advanced Open Water Class, we teach, would include the following dives, Search and Recovery, Navigation, Deep, Boat, and Wreck. Through the years, we have used the *Abbie Bursley* as the Wreck Dive for one of the five dives. In the fall of 1997, we were doing a wreck dive to complete an advanced open water course. We had set an anchor into the wreck and were waiting for slack high tide. John told our six students the story of what had happened to us a few years earlier while diving on the *Abbie Bursley*. We decided the best way to divide the group of six students was for us each to be in charge of a group of three students. Marlene would lead her students to the bow area of the wreck and John would start at the stern. We instructed the students to stay off the bottom so not to cause visibility issues. We had explained what to do if debris, or silt, was stirred by divers accidently hitting the bottom creating a black out effect. Students were told to hold onto part of the ship, rock or just the bottom; and wait for the cloud to pass. This assists with maintaining the buddy system and not having to surface to reunite. Marlene's group rolled out first and John's group gave them time to reach bottom and situate themselves on the wreck. John's group entered the water and dropped down into a kelp bed. They positioned themselves in a line and headed from stern to bow. Within a few kicks, they found some large timbers. Someone in Marlene's group apparently landed or was too close to the bottom with their fins and created turbidity, a dark cloud of silt. It drifted down in the current to John's group. When John noticed it coming towards them, he signaled to hold on to an object by grabbing his left wrist with his right hand. They all grabbed a solid object and waited for the silt cloud to pass. Before the silt cloud created the blackout situation, John looked down between two small beams. Looking back at him was a little white face. John thought, "Oh, what an eerie sight." He reached in between the beams and pick up a porcelain doll head. It suddenly became dark as the entire silt layer reached them. John knew that the visibility would clear in a few moments as the current would carry the silt layer down bay. The doll head looked so scary that it gave him a foolish idea. John decided that it was too good of an opportunity to let pass and not scare the living daylights out of one of his students. One of his advanced students was a 20 year old student by the name of Royce Gordon from Sorrento, Maine. He was a bright and ambitious learner and was an adventurous youth. He was a perfect student on which to deploy John's prank. John knew where Royce was because John had last seen him on John's left side. He had seen Royce grab an old beam after John had given the signal to hookup. While it was completely dark, John held the doll head in his right hand and put it in front of Royce's mask about a foot away. John knew wearing a black glove would make his hand appear to be invisible for a few seconds. John could see only a silhouette of Royce's head and could just barely make out his exhaust bubbles. While holding the doll's head a foot away from Royce's mask, John began moving it in and out. The visibility began to clear and John knew that Royce could see the doll's face. Royce's breathing became more vigorous. Royce was fixated on the little face and could not believe what he was seeing. John's black wetsuit glove was an excellent backdrop to make the little face look like it was suspended in darkness. Royce finally realized what he was observing and grabbed John's arm and shook his head from side to

Schooner Abbie Bursley

1880's German Porcelain Doll Head Recovered from the
Abbie Bursley

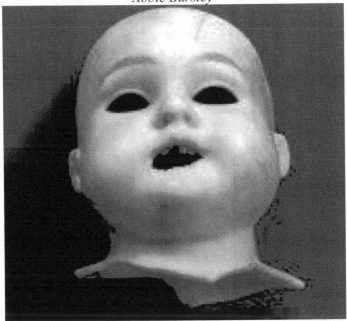

Daley Collection

side. John did not know when he had ever laughed so hard while diving. The groups finally ended the dive and boarded the boat. Royce was very unnaturally quiet. When all students were back aboard the boat, John told them about the incident. Everyone laughed hysterically, except Royce. John asked him, why are you so quiet. Royce said, "When I saw the little face, what ran through my mind at the time, was it must have been the ghost of the *Abbie Bursley* that had held Marlene and you against the bottom and it had come back for me!"

The 1880's Bisque German Porcelain Doll Head that was recovered from the *Abbie Bursley* was identified by Roberta Cunningham, a doll collector from Hancock, Maine. She said she could tell the origin of the doll by the way it was constructed and how the teeth were placed. Her and her husband, Rich, are members of the Sullivan Sorrento Historical Society as well as the Hancock Historical Society.

Schooner William Gillum

The schooner *William Gillum*'s construction was finished in August of 1864. She was built in Middletown, Connecticut. She was surveyed as being 191 tons, 98 foot long, 27 foot breadth, 7 foot depth and a draft of 8 feet. The *Gillum* was constructed of oak and cedar. She was fastened with galvanized iron. The owner and captain was H. Dickenson. During her lifetime, the schooner *William Gillum* called Haddam, and Middletown, Connecticut, as well as Portland and Sullivan, Maine, her homeports at different times during her sailing years.

She was constructed with hopes of acquiring government contracts to assist in the Civil War. This vision was a goal of nearly all ship owners during this time period. With the war ending in April 1865, the contracts such as these were not as readily available and those that were available were more competitive to obtain. The *Gillum* participated in the normal sea trade. The schooner traveled up and down the east coast with cargoes of the day and would turn a profit if the wind and weather cooperated. She carried loads of lumber, ice, coal, petroleum, fish, lime, guano, iron, granite, and general merchandise. Captain Dickenson held ownership of the *Gillum* until 1880 with several other captains assisting with her travels along the eastern seaboard. Captain Scoville and Captain Emmons were at the helm at various occasions during the period of 1867 to 1870. Captain J. J. Mehaffe not only skippered the *William Gillum* but from 1871 to 1877, was a consignee on some of the voyages. Captain Rogers commanded for the year of 1873. In 1881, the schooner *William Gillum* was sold to J. E. Leonard, who maintained ownership until 1885. He hired Captain Bacon to tend the helm for one year. Then Leonard hired Captain Pease to replace Captain Bacon for the years 1882 and 1883. In 1884, Captain Clark was given the helm. In 1885, Captain William Rase becomes the owner of the *William Gillum* and shares the captain duties with Captain Clark. He retained ownership until the *William Gillum* was sold to Captain John Carroll in 1889. Captain Carroll retained ownership through 1891. During the year 1890, Captain Conway worked for Captain Carroll. In 1891,

Schooner William Gillum

Captain Carroll sold the *William Gillum* to the Dunbar Bros. of Sullivan, Maine. Captain Carroll stayed on as the captain for the next five years.

During the years that the *Gillum* sailed, she was associated with a great deal of adventure and controversy. She became famous during a federal case involving maritime law. It covered the legality of restitution for cargoes jettisoned for the safety of the crew. The simple and consistent rule of law was that if the master carries a deck load without the consent of the shipper, the risk was the ship's responsibility. This was a long established practice.

In September of 1872, District Court D Massachusetts was the setting for the legal battle. The Honorable Judge John Lowell presided over Case No. [17,693]. The *Gillum* was carrying a cargo of 200 tons of pig iron to be delivered from Philadelphia for the Bay State Iron Company located in Boston. The *Gillum's* crew placed 50 tons of pig iron on the deck. The rest had been placed below deck. During a gale, the schooner was blown upon a reef. The captain decided to jettison 33 tons of the cargo from the deck. He

Schooner William Gillum

surmised this would save the rest of the load, the ship, and its crew. Consequently, the *Gillum* was able to free herself and continue on into port. The libellants, Bay State Iron Company, wanted to be reimbursed for the loss of 33 tons of pig iron that was thrown overboard to save the ship. The attorney for the owners of the *Gillum* argued that it was common practice to carry part of a deck load that was not perishable on the deck as long as it made the vessel easier to handle, which is generally safer in rough seas. T. K. Lothrop and A. Lincoln were the attorneys for the libellants. They concurred, but argued that when a load is carried on deck weighing more than 1/8 to 1/4 of the cargo, the underwriter for the ship must be notified, which was not done. They, also, stated that it is the expense of the vessel to insure any cargo above the deck.

Judge Lowell was presented with numerous precedent cases on both sides. After weighing through the legality, his final decision was that the libellants should recover their cost. The *Gillum* had responsibility to the Bay State Iron Company for the entire load. The *Gillum* had agreed that they were liable for the loss, but at a lower amount. The judge said that the *Gillum* should have made this offer before going to court. Judge Lowell allowed the Bay State Iron Company to bill for more than the loss of 33 tons. He stated, that the Supreme Court allowed, in this type of case, for the recovery of a general average loss. This exceeded the amount of iron that was jettisoned by the *Gillum*.

The *Gillum* seemed to be drawn to predicaments of this sort. On August 4, 1890, the *Gillum* with Captain Conway in charge went aground on Shovel Shoal, which is located off Chatham, Massachusetts, near Monomoy Point. She was transporting a load of lumber from Bangor, Maine, to Dennisport, Massachusetts, for S. S. Barker & Company. The crew jettisoned some of the cargo as to free themselves from the ledge. The owners of the *Gillum* argued that the wreck happened due to the ledge warning buoy being out of position. The vessel made it into port, but was leaking and pumps had to be manned.

In 1892, the Dunbar Bros. owned the ship and the *Gillum* called Sullivan, Maine her homeport.

Schooner William Gillum

The Dunbar Bros. were involved with different businesses. Harvey Dunbar, a junior member of the Dunbar Bros., had been in the coal business since 1886. He was originally with the Bar Harbor Coal Company, which later became the Clark Coal Company and he maintained his interests. The Dunbar Bros. owned a general merchandise store located in Sullivan Harbor. They also leased several quarries and organized crews to cut stone.

They eventually opened their own quarry in 1901. The *Gillum* carried cargoes of granite from Sullivan and returned with coal and merchandise for their store. The Dunbar's owned a stone wharf in Taunton Bay where they would load the stone and unload other cargo. On one occasion in 1895, a horse team carrying a load of granite was being backed onto the wharf. The wagon loaded with stone went too far back and fell into the bay. The horses were harnessed to the wagon and could not escape. They drowned between the *William Gillum* and the wharf.

In 1896, the *Gillum* was sailed onto the Hancock shore in Taunton Bay to have needed repairs completed. They attempted to make the repairs, but it was decided her needs were too great. With little hope of financial rewards, they abandoned the schooner. It is now resting below the Hancock Riverside Cemetery almost directly across the bay from the wrecked schooner *Abbie Bursley*.

Diving on the Schooner William Gillum

John had a conversation one summer day in 1996 with Tomcat Gordon. As it has been previously stated, Tomcat was a long time lobsterman who fished the waters of Taunton, Egypt, Hog and Frenchman's Bays. He told John that the *William Gillum* had been in a Hancock cove for a long time. He stated that when he was young, he would go over on the Hancock shore and dig blood worms and sometimes, on super low tides, he would dig next to the skeleton of the old schooner. At the high water mark, the *Gillum* sits in about ten

Schooner William Gillum

feet of water. At an exceptionally low tide, she is exposed for a very short period of time.

After becoming certified PADI instructors, further training and writing the Underwater Archaeology Specialty Course Program which had to be approved through PADI, we have taught the course at UMM as well as through private classes. The field school involved seven full days of diving on single or multiple wreck sites. The work involved searching, surveying, photographing, documenting, and sometimes recovering and preserving artifacts for display.

Offering Underwater Archaeology is a great fit for UMM due to the location of the University and with all of the maritime history in the Machias and Downeast areas. The first naval engagement of the American Revolutionary War was between the *HMS Margaretta* and the coastal, schooner *Unity*. The battle took place on June 12, 1775, off Machiasport, Maine. Not only is there factual history, these areas are full of maritime lore which consists of Vikings ships and pirates. There are many tales about the Downeast area possibly being the location of some of the treasure belonging to Pirate Bellamy.

In the summer of 2011, we were able to offer an Underwater Archaeology Field School. This time we decided to devote the entire seven days to finding some of the wreck sites that were not located to date. We have a personal policy by which if a person takes a diving course from us he or she never will have to pay for the same course again and may dive with us at his or her own risk during any repeated level course. We believe that this continues to reinforce safe diving practices. We have had numerous students take advantage of our policy. The summer of 2011 was no exception. Harry Fish Jr. had been a student in the 2003 Underwater Archeology Field School. However, Harry is more than a student; he is now a PADI Assistant Instructor and a great seaman who has sailed the North Atlantic and the Caribbean on many occasions. We had heavily recruited him as a student in the initial class because of his knowledge and expertise. Since the 2003 class was a great success, he offered to be involved with the 2011 session. Harry offered to use his boat, the 17 foot *Sundance*. He was accompanied by a PADI Divemaster, his nephew, Aaron Herzog. Aaron had been diving since he was twelve years old and completed the Underwater Archeology class and pool sessions. He has a strong nautical sense, has solid diving skills, and wanted to add to his diving resume. We used our 20 foot Eastport lobster boat. Other students that were involved were Dean Smith of Franklin, Maine, Scott Bickford of Harrington, Maine, Paul Savoy, of Sullivan, Maine, as well as Keith and Kevin VanGorden from New Hampshire. We were excited to be working with such a fine group of students on such a challenging adventure.

The dive schedule was set and during one of the days we hoped to solve a mystery. One of the photographs on the Maine History Website was of a wreck that was located in Sullivan. Its caption is, "Shipwreck on the Shore of Taunton Bay". We believed at first this wreck was most likely the *Abbie Bursley*. We studied the photograph and realized that the identification was not possible, because the *Bursley* was in deeper water. We then

Schooner William Gillum

Shipwreck on the Shore of Taunton Bay
Circa 1915

Courtesy Sullivan Sorrento Historical Society Picture taken by Sullivan native, Thomas C. Moon

noticed that the contour of the shoreline did not match the shoreline where the *Bursley* sank. In the picture near the bow of the wreck, there is a large rock on the beach. We used Google Earth photographs to search for the rock and a similar shoreline. Many times an outline of the skeleton of a shipwreck can be seen in Google Earth photographs. We spotted one not on the Sullivan shore but on the Hancock shore. It was where Tomcat had told John that he believed the old schooner *William Gillum* was located. We took our team of divers and at first tried to locate the wreck during high tide. We followed the pictures from Google Earth and from the Maine History Website.

Schooner William Gillum

Keith, Kevin, Aaron, Paul, and Marlene began the dive. In no time at all, in about ten feet of water, they located the remains of the schooner. Paul rose out of the water and exclaimed, "We have found deck planks!" The *Gillum* had been sheared off and what remained of her was a slight relief above the muddy, sandy bottom. Over the years, ice flows from out of Egypt, Hog and Taunton Bays caused most of the damage. Two major destructive forces that are prevalent on a shipwreck are chemical and mechanical deterioration. These major factors working in unison had basically taken an old ship and had eliminated most of its nautical structure. Some of the vessel is buried into the bottom. In a little over 115 years, the *Gillum* was nothing more than a few old timbers sticking out of the bottom of the Hancock shoreline. One can only imagine what will remain if left alone to its own demise in the next 115 years. One might argue that the *Gillum* is not historically important. We believe it is crucial in the realm of local history as well as in maritime law. Ships, like the *William Gillum*, created our history and maritime laws. Our forefathers sailed ships like her all over the world exporting and importing various goods. The *Gillum* is an important part of our local history and saving a piece of her before she is totally gone allows there to be a tangible part of history available for all to see and touch.

To do preservation on a large scale is expensive. Many underwater archeologists believe that it is best, when possible, to leave a shipwreck in situ preservation. This can be a fallacy if the conditions of where the wreck lies are too inhospitable for the ship to last. The theory of in situ is that the wreck will deteriorate to a certain point and that its concretion will help preserve its remains. This is somewhat true if the wreck is in deeper water. The wreck can then be disturbed at a later time when it is financially affordable to do the preservation. The wrecks in Taunton Bay are in shallow water having high oxygen content that speeds the deterioration process. The *William Gillum* is in shallow water no deeper than ten feet during high tide. During exceptionally low tides, it is exposed to the air. Ice masses during the spring drag across her remains.

Schooner William Gillum

The current is strong at times in this area and many of the artifacts that have been loosened by the changing of the tides are swept away.

We informed the students to remove the best looking plank they could find so we could put it into preservation. Depending on what type of material from which an object is constructed will determine what type of preservation method will be needed. The plank they chose was made from oak. It was placed in a fresh water bath for two years. Then, polyethylene glycol, PEG, was used to cover the plank to slow deterioration and preserve it.

Plank from the *William Gillum*

Daley Collection

Mining the Sullivan Lode

Mining Map 1881

Daley Collection/W.F. Stewart

Key:
#1 Swan Mine #2 Franklin Mine & Extension #3 Frenchman's
Bay Mine #4 Clark Mine & Extension
#5 Egypt Mine #6 Custer Mine & Extension #7 Cline Mine #8
Portland & Sullivan Mine
#9 Sullivan Falls Mine #10 Millbrook Mine #11 Ashley Mine
#12 Beacon Hill Mine #13 Morancy Mine
#14 Early Dawn Mine #15 Ford Mine #16 Bean Mine #17
Flanders Mine # 18 Copper Harbor Prospect Mine # 19 King
Gold Mine, location unknown

(Salem & Sullivan Mine aka Eureka Mine, Huronian Mine aka
Hagan Mine, and Harvey Elliot Mine aka Robert Emmett
Mine.)

The Metallix Company of America states there
were three major Silver Rushes in America. The
first was the Nevada Silver Boom of 1870 to 1879,

Mining the Sullivan Lode

which was also known as the Comstock Lode. The second was the Colorado Silver Boom from 1877 to 1893, after silver was discovered near the city of Leadville. The third was the Maine Silver Boom from 1878 to 1882, after silver was first discovered in Sullivan, Maine in 1877.

In 1878, the Bland-Allison Act required the U.S. Treasury to buy a certain amount of silver. This act was put forth by the United States Congress to have the U.S. Treasury make silver a bimetal currency with gold. The theory was that silver dollars would be circulated and, consequently, a silver demand would be developed. Having silver become a demand would allow for inflation due to having more currency available. With more currency available, this would assist western farmers in paying off their debt to the banks. The farmers would be able to charge more for their products; thus, creating more income to pay on their debt. President Rutherford B. Hayes vetoed the Bland-Allison Act but congress was able to obtain enough support to override his veto. President Hayes was angry over Congress's actions and decided to order the U.S. Treasury to buy only small amounts of silver. Finally, in 1890, the Sherman Silver Purchase Act replaced the Bland-Allison Act. It forced the government to purchase more silver for the U.S. Treasury. The price of silver dropped. In 1890, one ounce of silver was worth $1.16 and by 1894 it was worth $0.60 an ounce. U.S. citizens lost confidence in silver as a metal for currency. People were requesting that banks provide payments only in gold or gold certificates. This caused a depletion of the U.S. Treasury's gold reserves. President Grover Cleveland led the repeal of the Sherman Silver Purchase Act. This repeal of the act demonetized silver and made gold the only metallic standard in the United States.

In 1877, silver was discovered in Sullivan, Maine. It was first spotted by Mr. A. A. Messer on a ledge out in the bay near the ferry crossing. The silver was mostly contained in a natural mineral called galena, which is made up of lead with silver content as high as 2 percent. Speculation ran as high as $200 a ton in silver and $20 to the ton in gold.

Mining the Sullivan Lode

Gold and Silver Prices of 1880
Price of 1 oz. of Gold $ 20.67
Price of 1 oz. of Silver $ 1.00
Brick of Silver Weight 62 lbs.
Miners Pay for an 8 Hour Day in Sullivan, Maine $1.25

above ground $1.50 below ground.

Gold and Silver Prices of 2017
Price of 1 oz. of Gold $1300.00
Price of 1 oz. of Silver $17.00
Average Wage of Labor for 8 hour day $100.00
Cost to process one ton of ore at the Sullivan Mill in
1881was $11.00 a ton
Assay of Silver per ton of Pay Ore $20.00 to $200.00
Daley Collection

In 1878, the Maine State Legislature became active in creating laws to assist fledgling mining companies to help benefit the business of mining. Such laws were, "Section I: That all mines of gold, silver or of the baser metals, which are now, or may be opened and in the process of development, shall be exempt from taxation for a term of ten years from the time of such opening. Section II: This act shall not affect the taxation of the land of the surface improvements of the same, at the same rate of valuation as similar lands and buildings in the vicinity." This act prevented the possibility of local tax assessors of placing excessive valuations on the property and the mining equipment. This act made

Mining the Sullivan Lode

it so the land and buildings had to be taxed at the same rate as land and buildings throughout the towns. Nothing slows business growth quicker than over taxation.

The mining king of the area was Mr. Francis Worcester. He was the first man to bring mining interest into the area. In 1878, he was financially broke, but after the discovery of silver, he was able to recruit enough investors to back the opening of the first mine in Sullivan. He named his venture the Sullivan Mine. He obtained and held leases on

The West Sullivan Mining District
Circa 1881

Courtesy Maine Historic Preservation Commission.

approximately 35,000 acres of land in the area. This business move made it so all new mines had to make terms with him before they could open. He privately owned the Millbrook Mine located by present day Gray Brook. He also opened an office

Mining the Sullivan Lode

in Sullivan to help promote the development of mining in the area.

We have identified 19 separate mining companies formed within the Town of Sullivan Mining District in 1883. Their names are Flanders Mine, Portland-Sullivan Mine, King Gold Mine, Faneuil Hall & Sullivan Mine, Waukeag Mine, Sullivan Mine, Bean Mine, Pine Tree Mine, Milton Mine, Salem Sullivan Mine, Richmond Mine, Sullivan Falls Mine, Millbrook Mine, Ashley Mine, Copper Harbor Prospect Mine, Beacon Hill Mine, Boss of the Bay Mine, Golden Circle Mine and Morancy Mine. Most of these mines were located on the shorelines or within a few hundred feet of the shorelines of Taunton Bay, Frenchman's Bay, and Flanders Bay, which created the shoreline of the mining district. The present day towns of Sullivan and Sorrento were known as Sullivan during that time period. In 1895 the Town of Sorrento was established. The companies primarily mined for silver, gold, and copper. Silver being the commodity mined in the majority of the mines. They did obtain a byproduct of gold from the iron pyrite, referred to as fool's gold. Within the iron pyrite, there is a small percentage of real gold.

The Golden Circle Mine was considered primarily a gold mine and was located on Seward's Island, which is present day Treasure Island in Sorrento, Maine. The Golden Circle Mine closed around 1883 and was reopened in the year 1900 for a short period of time. The company had trouble with saltwater in the mine because it was located on a very narrow peninsular of the island. The saltwater was seeping into the shafts, causing the expense of pumping the water out and repairing/replacing damaged equipment due to the water containing salt.

When headed west in Taunton Bay, the next adjoining bay is Egypt Bay, which lines the towns of Hancock and Franklin. In these towns, we identified nine companies formed to obtain silver and copper. Their names were Cline, Custer (also known as the Copperopolis), Robert Emmett, Hagan, Clark, Frenchman's Bay, Franklin, Swan, and B. F. Butler. On the shores of Egypt Bay in the towns of Hancock and Franklin, these mines were

Mining the Sullivan Lode

similar to the mines along the Sullivan side of Taunton Bay. They were primarily dug within one hundred feet of the high tide mark. Two exceptions were in Franklin the Swan, which was located off of the Great Pond Road and the B. F. Butler, which was located next to George's Pond. Several of these mines only had one shaft. They proceeded in this manner for financial reasons. The mines started having air quality issues due to not having enough air exchange to remove the dust. Since the miners were breathing in the dust particles, created from drilling quartz and silica, many of the miners were developing silicosis. Silicosis is a lung disease that is caused by inhaling small particles of rocks, sand and silica. It is more commonly referred as "Rocks in the Box". They may have been misdiagnosed as having pneumonia or tuberculosis due to the symptoms being similar. The only way to improve the situation is to remove the miners from the poor quality of air or to increase the air exchange which will remove a lot of the particles and provide breathable air. Many mines tried to address the issue with drilling second shafts. These shafts would be connected in order to create a chimney affect to assist with improving air quality in the main shafts. With crosscut shafts joining the main shafts, air flow exchange would take place more readily and particles would be drawn out of the main shaft.

Advertisement for Equipment

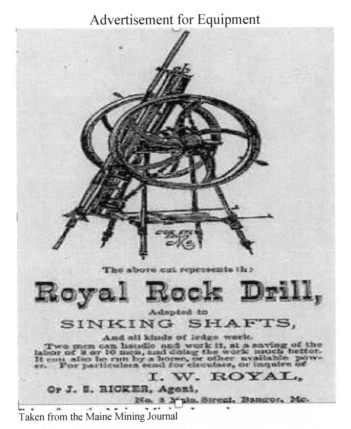

The above cut represents the

Royal Rock Drill,

Adapted to

SINKING SHAFTS,

And all kinds of ledge work.

Two men can handle and work it, at a saving of the labor of 8 or 10 men, and doing the work much better. It can also be run by a horse, or other available power. For particulars send for circulars, or inquire of

I. W. ROYAL,

Or J. S. RICKER, Agent,

No. 2 Main Street, Bangor, Me.

Taken from the Maine Mining Journal

About 60% of the employees hired by the local quarries as well as in the mines were immigrants.

Mining the Sullivan Lode

The largest groups were made up of Scotsmen and Canadians, and the smaller groups were made up of Englishmen and Irishmen. Many of the miners lived in boarding houses where they received their room and board as part of their salaries. The Milton Mine was the largest of all the mines and advertised that the men could have hot and cold running showers after an eight hour workday. The Milton Mine, also, provided work pants for their employees. Levi &Straus pants were purchased as waist overalls known as jeans. What made these garments unique were the material used and the copper fasteners on the pockets. The actual denim was produced in the Amoskeag Manufacturing Company in Manchester, New Hampshire. People were able to obtain these jeans from Levi & Strauss in either blue or brown colors. The term, blue jeans, comes from the indigo blue color of the blue trousers and from the pants being made out of jean material. These colors allowed for dirt not to show as easily. The jeans were fastened with copper buttons in front.

Stock was sold from private and incorporated

mines with the state allowing up to 100,000 shares to be sold per mine. A typical price for a stock was between three and five dollars per share. Most of the mines were owned by outside interests from Portland or Boston. The mines were generally under the leadership of a president, secretary, and superintendent. They were all responsible to the stockholders. The general everyday operations were under the supervision of the superintendent. The superintendent would be on site and give the orders for the day. Some of the mines were large enough to have what they referred to as the head engineer. He would make out the work schedules and collaborate with the superintendent as to what drifts and veins to blast and excavate. With assistance from the engineer, the superintendent would determine the progression of the mine based on the direction of the drifts and the availability of men. The larger mines like the Milton Mine, Waukeag Mine, and Sullivan Mine, had three work shifts that ran 6 days a week for 8 hours per day. The only day on which they did not operate was Sunday.

Mining the Sullivan Lode

(L to R) Lifting Works Waukeag Mine, Knights of Pythias
Hall, and Tug Phillip S. Eaton
Circa 1900

Courtesy Sullivan Sorrento Historical Society

They also had a real problem with the availability of men working in the mines due to seasonal requirements at home to prepare for the cold winters. During the haying season, a lot of the employees refused to work in the mines until the hay was gathered for winterfeed. During this time, many of the schooners that took granite and mined ore in the spring from Sullivan returned with coal for the steam engines. Due to men working their farms, the company may not have enough men available to unload the coal.

Mining the Sullivan Lode

All of the mines were considered hard rock mines having little risk of cave-ins and had water problems. They turned into large artesian wells when the pumps were not operated on Sunday. On

Water Draining on Right Side of Shaft Draining Back to the Sump

Courtesy Denver Public Library

Monday, the pumps had to be run for at least half a day in order for the water to be pumped out of the shafts. Some of the larger mines would have their engineers start the pumps on Sunday afternoons, so the water would be pumped out for the first shift of workers. This condition was made worse during the winter due to the machines being in buildings that were not insulated well and this could cause these machines to freeze and break. The mines had to be pumped before any work could be completed and this became costly as well as a nuisance to the companies. However, this was not always a bad issue. The mines could use the water to assist with running the steam engines and the excess water was pumped into the bay. It was actually helpful since they needed a fresh water source for their steam engines. Several of the mines built dams on small streams, such as Grays Brook, and then would pipe the water using gravity feed to the mine to be used for the steam engines.

Steam Engine

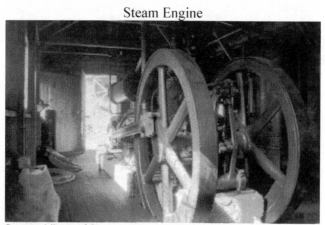

Courtesy Library of Congress

Most of the shafts were driven in a vertical angle. It was much easier to remove the ore than with the shafts in an inclined position. The vertical shafts were driven plumb and the use of the lifting works made it much simpler due to not having to deal with the friction from the wheels of the carts to remove the materials. Most of the secondary vertical shafts were dug to assist with ventilation. All of the drifts from the main vertical shaft were slanted slightly upward. This allowed the water to drain from the drift to the main vertical shaft and into the sump, which was a holding reservoir at the bottom of the main shaft. The sump was where the

Miners Searching for Pay Streak
Circa 1880

Courtesy Denver Public Library

pumps were placed to lift the water up and out of the mine. The piping that was used was made of

Mining the Sullivan Lode

twisted metal bands with asbestos lining wrapped around the outside. It was mounted on the sides of the main shaft going from the sump to the top of the shaft. The main shafts were timbered and braced with large six and eight inch thick square beams.

The expense of mining in Sullivan, Maine was on the average reasonably cheap compared to the prices of material and labor in other areas of the United States. In Sullivan, cordwood could be purchased at $2.50 per cord, coal at $7.84 per ton delivered and lumber at $7.00 per thousand board feet. A miner could be employed for $1.25 for an eight hour day if he stayed at the surface and $1.50 a day if he went underground. The food was considered cheap because Sullivan was regarded as a successful agricultural district. Steamboats could easily provide transportation to Boston via Portland three times a week for needed mining supplies. Schooners were abundant for necessary cargo trips such as for coal, lumber or the transportation of rich ore.

The Milton Mine owners operated the company sawmill for the purpose of producing lumber to be used for mining. They sold lumber supplies to other mines. The shafts were timbered with wood from local sawmills. The timbers that were placed on the sides of the shaft had several purposes. The timbers gave the water pipe something to be mounted to and they helped with keeping debris from falling into the shaft.

Suction pumps were not used for they were only effective to 30 feet. The plunger pumps were used and had pushing pistons that basically pushed the water out of the shaft. Air from the compressor powered the pumps. Steam engines powered the compressors and the lifting works. The rock drill was operated by compressed air. The ore buckets

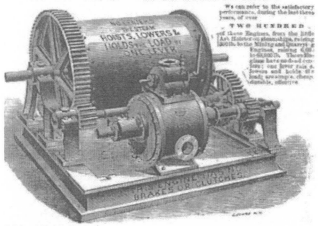

Maine Mining Journal

or ore cart had wheels on the bottom so they could be pushed along after they were disconnected from the lifting works. They were pushed on a set of rails to and from the drifts or crosscuts to the shafts.

Bucket with Wheels Used for Transporting Men & Ore

Courtesy History Colorado Center

The rails within the Sullivan mines were made from oak. When the rocks were hoisted to the surface they were assayed and distributed to either a dump

184

pile or process pile. To be permitted into the process pile, the ore had to be determined to have a profitable amount of silver or gold. Some of the mines used farm animals such as donkeys to pull the carts filled with ore to the chosen dump pile. The main vertical shaft was divided in the middle. Most of the main shafts were cut nine feet by four feet and separated by a wooden wall making for a two-way shaft, four feet by four and a half feet. This allowed for up and down transportation of men and ore at the same time. The ladders used in the shafts were of a split rail design and was made with pine rails and oak rungs. The ladders would be placed in the shaft to be used as needed as well as for emergency exits. As the digging of shaft progressed, a ladder would be placed in the shaft. When the shaft reached the height of the ladder, the ladder would be attached to the support beam and another ladder would be added. When the shaft reached the height of the second ladder, that ladder would be attached to meet the first ladder, and so on. All mines had these emergency escape ladders mounted in one of their vertical shafts. This was to

Mining the Sullivan Lode

be used in case of an emergency such as a breakdown in the lifting works.

The lifting works had a steel cable that went through a gallows frame to a winch powered by a steam engine. The gallows frame was placed over the top of the shaft in a plumb position so buckets or carts that were lowered or raised within the shaft would not come in contact with the walls. Buckets/carts carried men, tools, ore, blasting wire, dynamite and any other necessary mining equipment.

Steam engines were a necessity for the bigger mines, but it was common for horses or oxen to be used as their primary form of energy in the smaller mines. Steam engines were powered by coal or wood. The steam engines powered the air compressors which ran the drills, winches, and the pumps.

In the smaller mines, a whim system was used due to it being simple to operate and cheaper to run. A whim or sometimes called a whin, was a winch system. A horse or oxen would be used to turn the winch which in turn would raise or lower the bucket

Mining the Sullivan Lode

A Horse Powered Whin

within the shaft. Since most of the mines had access to horses from local farms, the horses were readily available. The horses were used for their power to operate the whim, when the shaft was deeper and it was harder to remove the materials by hand. As the mine shaft became deeper, it would not be uncommon to use more than one horse or oxen to operate the whin.

There were lots of dangers in working in the mines. Most of the mining companies paid higher wages to workers who worked underground due to the dangers. Some of the hazards came from steam engine malfunctions, boiler explosions, burns from

187

the furnaces, falls through ladder holes, falling rocks, drowning, and premature dynamite explosions.

The miners did not wear helmets for head protection but wore flannel or wool hats. They carried a sticking tommie for lighting, which was an iron pin with a candleholder. The men would be working underground using only the light provided from the sticking tommie. Most of the sticking tommies were made by the local or the mine's blacksmith. It had a picked point, which could be hooked on a hat or driven in a wooden beam or crevice within the rock. At this time, the men

Candle Holder, 1880 Sticking Tommie, Miner's Lightning Wore on Their Hat

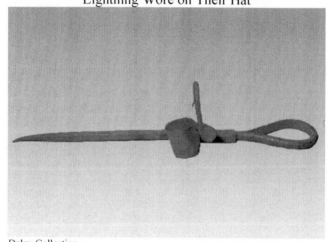

Daley Collection

choose to use sticking tommies and not lanterns because the lanterns use more oxygen to burn and left an odor within the mine as they burned.

Other hazards of working within the mines were lack of clean air and low oxygen levels. This type of hard rock mining created many suspended fine particles within the air. Breathing in this contaminated air caused lung disease for miners called silicosis. Silica, commonly found in quartz, would become airborne due the using air drills to pulverize the ore and from dynamite blasting of the

Dynamite Advertisement

GIANT POWDER

(DYNAMITE.)

The attention of miners is invited to this standard explosive as being the best in the market.

Information, Prices, Etc.

furnished by

GEO. A. GOODYEAR,

Agent Atlantic Giant Powder Company,

15 Central St., Boston.

Courtesy Maine Mining Journal

Mining the Sullivan Lode

rock within the cut. Some of the miners chose minimal protection from exposure to the airborne silica by wrapping a wet cloth around their faces while drilling. Dynamite was an extreme danger from a host of directions. The inexperienced or the careless act could be deadly. To increase the ore production, it was not uncommon for men working in one drift or cut to blast while men would be working in another drift or cut. Sometimes, static electricity would ignite the dynamite prematurely.

A universal bell system was used in all the mines. It allowed miners that were employed with different mines at the same time or that would transfer from one mine to another to have a common sounding system. A line was hung from the gallows to the bottom of the shaft. Miners could sound the alarm at top of the shaft by pulling on the line. An engineer would answer the miners below by raising the rope a said distance to notify the miners he was waiting for a response. The bell tender was the only person who shall ring the bell to communicate with the engineer. He was in charge of the lifting works and the rate it would raise the bucket or cart. There was only one exception to this rule and that was if an emergency arose. The person notifying the engineer what level of emergency was happening did so by how many times the bell would ring. This was called the uniform code of mine signals.

The uniform code bell system was:

- 1-bell, stop
- 2-bells, lower
- 3-bells, hoist
- 4-bells, lower men
- 5-bells, hoist men
- 6-bells, blasting signal
- 7-bells, turn on or off steam
- 8-bells, turn on or off air
- 9-bells, danger signal
- 10 bells, meant there was a fire.

Courtesy Maine Mining Journal

Pine Tree Silver Mining Company

Pine Tree Silver Mining Company
Circa 1881

Courtesy Maine Historic Preservation Commission

The Pine Tree Silver Mining Company started its private operation in the Spring of 1879, and employed 17 men. The company was incorporated on January 28, 1880, and made a change in its corporation guidelines to increase to five directors on March 15, 1880. The mine had General John Murray Corse from New York as its president. They had W. O. Arnold as secretary, who was from Bangor. Robert L. Cutting Jr., of New York, was elected treasurer. Mr. E. G. Johnston was hired as

192

Pine Tree Silver Mining Company

the mining engineer/superintendent. Colonel Charles H. Lewis was a primary owner and one of the directors of the Pine Tree Mine. He had been a Union Officer involved in the Southern Campaign during the Civil War. This is where he met General Corse. The Pine Tree Mine was allowed to sell up to 100,000 shares of stock for five dollars a share. The mine owned almost 700 feet on the Sullivan Lode.

General Corse was a Union Civil War officer who became famous after the battle of Allatoona in October of 1864. He had 2,100 men under his command and he was given the order by General William Tecumseh Sherman to stand his ground. General Sherman said these famous words, "Hold on, I am coming!" A popular ballad was written about his actions at Allatoona called "Hold the Fort, for I am coming." General Corse and his men held off nearly 7,000 Confederate Troops under the command of General John Bell Hood. General Corse lost a third of his men and was severely wounded. He was struck by shrapnel in the face and lost his right cheekbone and a third of his ear.

Pine Tree Silver Mining Company

Gen. John Murray Corse, President, Pine Tree Mine

Courtesy Library of Congress

He was able to recover enough to resume command of his troops. Later in his career, he was under the command of General Sherman in the campaign, March to the Sea, and the battle, Siege of Savannah. He moved to Winchester, Massachusetts and was appointed the postmaster of Boston. He was elected as the chairman of the State's Democratic Committee. He married the grandniece of former

Pine Tree Silver Mining Company

U.S. President Franklin Pierce, from New Hampshire.

The Pine Tree Silver Mine was located between the Milton Mining Company and the Sullivan Mining Company on the shore of Taunton Bay. A cofferdam was built to help prevent bay water from entering the shaft. The mine shaft was excavated in hopes of hitting the Sullivan Lode. The company invested a great some of money in the construction of the mine.

(L to R) Wooden Fence around Pine Tree Shaft, Cofferdam, Randy Mosley, Circa 2017

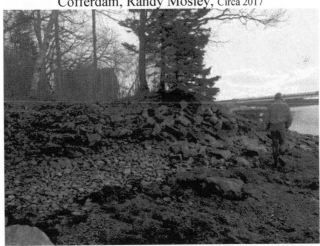

Daley Collection

The Pine Tree Mine offered 20,000 shares of stock on the market at five dollars a share. The mining works consisted of a large shaft house,

Pine Tree Silver Mining Company

which was 65 feet by 24 feet with a wing of 27 feet by 20 feet attached. In the basement of the wing, the boilers were set. Over the boiler room, two rooms were fitted for an office and the miners' sleeping quarters. A large gallows was constructed over the top of the shaft. It was one of the largest hoisting frames in the district and was designed to allow the mine to reach a depth of 600 feet. A water holding tank of 10,000 gallons was put in place. A dam was constructed about 650 feet from the mine on a small stream. Today, this stream runs next to the home owned by Pete Thomas of Sullivan, Maine. A two inch pipe was laid leading to the tank which provided water to all parts of the works. The pipe was buried five feet deep to prevent freezing during the winter months. A large wharf was constructed next to the mine to provide a location to load and unload ore and/or supplies. The Pine Tree Mine would store the ore on their new wharf, which would allow for less handling of the ore. The wharf had an 80 foot front and was extended out from shore where it could be used during high and low tides.

Pine Tree Silver Mining Company

Colonel C. H. Lewis was a spokesman and one of the directors of the Pine Tree Mine. He announced to all investors, they were going to ship their enriched ore to England to be treated. The company sent a representative to England to negotiate the price and to determine if this would be a more cost effective way to smelt the ore.

The vertical shaft was unique because it contained a three compartment shaft. Two of the compartments were 4 feet by 4½ feet on each side of the shaft. The third middle compartment was 3 feet by 4 ½ feet. The shaft descended to 66 feet where they struck the vein of silver. At this point, the miners excavated a 70 foot crosscut with 40 feet to the east and 35 feet to the west of the shaft, excavating part of the crosscut under the bay. The quality of the ore was not what they had hoped, so they decided to continue the shaft down to 126 feet. They dug another crosscut 30 feet out to the vein and made long drifts east and west on the vein. The majority of the mining was done at this level. The vein showed its greatest potential with a pay streak of rich ore of nearly 2 ½ feet.

Pine Tree Silver Mining Company

As in all of the mines, they had to install pumps to keep the shaft clear of water. It filled with water during the times the company was not able to run the pumps because of breakdowns, shutdowns, and/or waiting for money, men, and supplies.

Pine Tree Mine is encircled by the wooden fence.

Daley Collection

In May of 1881, the Pine Tree Mining Company decided a new superintendent was needed. This idea was brought to light because of inadequate attention to maintenance of the machinery which caused a machine to explode. It was feared that the machinery did malfunction because the incumbent superintendent was not overseeing the proper running and maintenance of the equipment. If the equipment was continually improperly maintained, someone may be injured or the mine would flood and all the workers would be laid off. If a miner was injured or the mine was not in operation, the company would lose money. The trustees felt that they needed to hire a new superintendent. The new superintendent chosen was A. A. Messer, the first mining engineer who discovered the Sullivan Lode in 1877. Messer was convinced that the Sullivan Lode had up to $200 of silver per ton in some of the ore. He felt the mine would be able to support a paying situation quickly as long as he received the financial backing from the directors. He needed to get the machinery and pumps back to a functioning state. Superintendent Messer ordered many improvements which included clapboards and a newly shingled roof for the shaft house. He knew that if investors came up to look at the mine, they needed to see a mine that was moving in the right direction. Sadly, the improvements he made were only cosmetic. In February of 1881, the directors put 3500 shares up for sale at $1 a share. By September of 1881, the company was selling stock

Pine Tree Silver Mining Company

at $.50 a share. The investors lost confidence because the value of the stock had substantially dropped. The mine was not able to acquire the new machinery needed to keep the operations running. The Pine Tree Mine closed in 1883 and never reopened.

Investigating the Pine Tree Mine

For many years while lobster fishing, we noticed a round small shaped point protruding out into the cove next to Gordon's Wharf. John believed it was the Pine Tree Mine shaft, but was not totally sure. We decided to investigate this location and search the area to see what remained of the old mining works. We searched the area and noticed an old granite and rock foundation and a water filled mineshaft. The shaft was dug on the shore near the high tide mark. A cofferdam surrounded the shaft and held back the bay water. The opening of the shaft was elevated about eight feet and was filled with fresh water. Freshwater spilled out over the top of the shaft and trickled down to the shore. We researched the mine's construction and underground works. At first, we were not exactly convinced the shaft was the Pine Tree Mine. We studied the 1881 Colby Atlas, and the mine appeared to line up with the map. We decided to measure the depth of the shaft. If the depth of the shaft was between 124 and 126 feet, it would most likely be the Pine Tree Mine. We used a set of old window weights, tied them to a 200 foot piece of floating warp line, and dropped the line down the shaft. When the weights landed on what we suspected to be the bottom of the shaft, we marked the line and carefully raised it so not to become entangled with any debris. Once out of the mine shaft, we measured it with a 100 foot tape measure. The mark on the rope measured exactly 125 feet. We believed at the bottom of the shaft sediment from leaves and falling rocks would account for about a foot of debris.

John remembered, as a young 12 year old boy, going down on Gordon's Wharf with a hand line to fish for flounder. He had not caught any fish and thought he would walk back along the shore, cut up across Gordon Cemetery to his Grandmother's, Jessie Daley's, house. She was known to many as Nannie. On this occasion, he decided to look into this shaft. John used his hand line to try and determine how deep the shaft was. He had left some old herring on the hook for he did not want to take the time to knock or pull it off. To his great surprise, he was able to reach the bottom of the shaft. Shortly after starting to reel the hand line in, a strong tug was felt. John was shocked and thought at first he must of have caught his hook on old trash in the mine. John noticed as he pulled it up it came relatively easy. Just before it reached the surface, he felt a series of pulls. He gave it a sharp yank and to his surprise, a giant eel about four feet long and as thick as his arm came to the surface. John is not a lover of eels! John retrieved his Kamp King Pocketknife and cut his line. The old eel slowly twisted and slithered itself back down the shaft. John never tried that again!

Years later, John and Marlene decided to investigate the shaft again. Marlene offered to scuba dive to the bottom of the shaft. She would stay on the down line, go straight down and then straight up, taking pictures along the way. The depth was at the maximum depth range for scuba, which is 130 feet for normal breathing air. We did not have any access to mixed gases nor did we have any experience using them. The shaft being a three compartment shaft would be a tight fit if the two of us attempted it at the same time and went within the same shaft compartment. Not knowing how far the wooden wall dividers went towards the bottom, we would not be able to take different compartments. The only way we would be able to stay together and to assist one another would be to follow each other in the same compartment. If we decided to attempt using different compartments, we would be isolated from each other and not be able to assist one another in an emergency. If we dived in the same compartment, the person who would be located above the other diver within would be in a mass of bubbles. That person could have issues maintaining buoyancy because the density of the water would change as the exhaust air bubbles rose. John felt the risk was light, but real, and John decided to dive alone. He had planned to descend on the down line to about 66 feet, never leave the line, take a few pictures of the crosscut, and swim back up the shaft. He did not intend to go to the bottom at 125 feet, at least not on the first dive. John felt that if everything went accordingly, Marlene and he would do the deeper dive at a later date.

On a warm summer day in July of 2003, John had his brother-in-law, Terry Theriault, from Chester, Maine, and his teenage son, Kris, lobster fishing with him. They had been hauling lobster gear for a couple of hours. At about 10 am, John asked them if they wanted to help him do a special dive. They were game, so John retrieved his dive gear. He also seized two Pelican Pro Underwater Dive Lights and a down line weighted with two iron window weights. To document this experience, John retrieved a 35mm Bonica Snapper Underwater Camera with a side mount strobe. They loaded the equipment into his boat at Gordon's Wharf and motored to the old cofferdam of the Pine Tree Mine. John tethered a line from the front of his boat to the big old oak tree on the shore.

One of the rules of diving is to "plan your dive and dive your plan." John planned to never leave the down line, go directly to the 66 foot level, take a couple of pictures and ascend via the line. He has completed more difficult and dangerous dives than this. He felt that the whole dive would last under 15 minutes. John was excited about the dive and the pictures that he would be taking. He was already anticipating success.

They carried his dive gear from the boat to the shaft opening. John lowered the window weights into the right side compartment with half inch red float line. The down line went to the bottom and John raised the weights up a few feet to prevent stirring the bottom sediment. He took the excess line and tied it to a small oak tree about ten feet from the shaft. He wore his blue Parkway Dry Suit for warmth and protection. It is a quarter inch neoprene suit with a zipper going from the middle of his back between his legs to the center of his chest. It has two valves on the chest area; one is a deflation button, which allows air out and the second valve has a low-pressure hose attached to the regulator which allows him to inflate the suit via the scuba tank. With a dry suit as a person descends, it will compress from the pressure and needs to be inflated to prevent a condition known as a squeeze. If you experience a squeeze in the suit, water may be drawn in around the seals or the suit pressure may draw blood to the surface of your skin and create an irritation called a hickey. John wore a weight belt consisting of 42 pounds of lead to assist with neutral buoyancy and used a red 80 cubic inch aluminum tank for his air supply. Each underwater light had a lanyard; he fastened one of the lights to his right foot and the other to left wrist. He laid on his belly and slowly slid backwards into the shaft. He did so in order to safely enter the water. The water was fresh, clean and fairly clear. He could feel the coolness of the water through his dry suit. He had debated on whether to wear his fins. John planned to pull himself slowly along the down line. He decided that it was safer to wear the fins than not in case the rope broke. He wore neoprene gloves for protection from the cold and suspected sharp objects that may be in the shaft. Just as he was deflating his suit to follow the line down, Terry passed him the camera. It was tethered to a lanyard, and he attached it on his right wrist. John turned on both lights and looked down the long dark shaft. He could clearly see about 30 feet as the light disappeared into darkness. The light shone off the compartment's old wooden walls. The wood that was in the mine was in excellent shape; cold, clean water preserves wood. He did not have any concern over the possibility of a cave-in. He figured, if this shaft had survived for over 120 years, it would survive for the next 15 minutes.

John made his way down the line trying to stay in the center of the compartment. He did not want to brush any sediment from the walls into the water. The only light within the shaft after the first few feet would be from what he was carrying. He had made his way down to about 10 feet when he stopped to equalize. John gazed up and down the shaft to evaluate his situation. He observed from the light attached to his foot that everything appeared to be the same as it was earlier when he entered the shaft. The water was clear and very dark below his light and resembled a tunnel. There was nothing for the light to reflect on other than the walls and the bottom stayed dark. John was breathing much harder than he realized and was creating a mass of bubbles above him. He held onto the down line tightly in his left hand. He started to have what he can only describe as an extreme anxiety problem. John had no idea what really caused his problem other than in the back of his mind, he was suppressing fear. He was anxious due to not knowing what was below him within the darkness. He closed his eyes and started kicking his fins and made his way back up the shaft. He allowed the down line to slip through his hand, grasping it once or twice to slow his ascent. Once he broke the surface, Terry exclaimed, "Wow! That was a fast trip!" John pulled his mask off and shook his head. John stated he was confused and for some reason he was having a mental issue and could not continue. Terry laughed and helped John out of the shaft. Terry and Kris helped John carry his gear back to the boat.

Pine Tree Silver Mining Company

To this day, John has no idea why this dive bothered him in such a way. He can only imagine that his mind created fears that were not real, and this caused the anxiety. John has laughed and told people that maybe he was thinking about that old eel he had caught in his younger years. He may have thought the eel was still living and growing in the mine shaft and waiting for him to return.

In reality, it is very dangerous to attempt such a dive without proper training. Marlene and John are certified to teach numerous specialties. Cave diving is not one of them. John has thought many times about this poster that is placed in front of cave openings warning divers to stay out unless properly trained. How true it is.

Faneuil Hall Mining Company

The Faneuil Hall Mine is located to the west of the Waukeag Mine on Taunton Bay. The mine is about 70 feet from the shore in front of Gordon Cemetery. In 1879, the property was purchased by two men and later shares were offered for sale to friends to help develop the company. In March of 1880, the company was formed due to the fact they were in need for some financial backing. The owner offered 2000 shares of stock at $2.00 a share to the public. The owners and their investors felt that the mine was going to be so successful they decided to buy all of the available stock. Seven men owned the Faneuil Hall Mine, which made this a private enterprise. They concluded this would allow the mine to develop rapidly by having shareholders instead of stockholders. The first officers of the Faneuil Hall Mine were Charles H. North of Somerville, Massachusetts, as president and L.A. Emery of Ellsworth, Maine, as the secretary.

The mine's shaft was started in June of 1880. The owners contracted John Reed, an old Cornish miner from Cornwall, England, to be superintendent. He had vast experience in this type

Faneuil Hall Mining Company

of mining. At first, the miners used a horse whim for power. Once the shaft got deeper than 50 feet it became too difficult to continue without machinery. The company bought a 50 horsepower double hoisting engine with two large boilers from Messrs. Beckett & McDowell. The hoisting works would enable the sinking of the shaft to a maximum depth of 1000 feet. It was able to hoist two tons of ore at a rate of 300 feet per minute. They used an Ingersoll Drill, which had its air supplied from a compressor built by George Blake Mfg. Company of Boston. The owners made contracts with private enterprises for a said amount of the shaft to be excavated. The Messrs. Joy & Murphy was one of the companies that was contracted to drill the shaft to fifty feet. The owners would then reevaluate the ore vein and do an assay. A decision would then be made as to whether or not to start a drift, issue another contract or to drill deeper. If they were happy with the work of the private contracted mining company, they could continue the contract based on affordability. The superintendent made day-to-day decisions. If a large sum of money was

Faneuil Hall Mining Company

needed for work in the mine, the superintendent would check with the president and he, in turn, would call a special board meeting with the officers to discuss availability of funds or how to continue to raise funds. The Faneuil Hall Mine held its annual meeting at the Waukeag House in Sullivan. This mine was somewhat unique in that the decisions could be quickly made with only seven owners.

The Faneuil Hall Mine was called on paperwork, the Faneuil Hall and Sullivan Mine. By April of 1881, the mine had a powerful complex of works. The first building was a small blacksmith shop. It was constructed for the purpose of making any fasteners or metal supports needed in the mine. A shaft house was built which was 83 feet by 30 feet in size with the easterly side of the building covering the shaft. The westerly side of the building contained the machine, engine, and boiler rooms; miners' apartments; and carpenter shop. Inside the machine shop was a double hoisting drum made by Messrs. Kendall & Roberts which had two 50 horsepower boilers.

Faneuil Hall Mining Company

In 1881, the Faneuil Hall Mining Company hired A. A. Hayward to take over the position of superintendent. Mr. Hayward had his money invested in the mine and decided to build himself a cottage about two hundred feet to the west of the shaft. He knew that it would be best to live near the mine to make it easier for him to run the everyday operations. Piping from the shaft house to the cottage was laid to provide the cottage with heat and water.

The Faneuil Hall had two openings but only one

Faneuil Hall Mining Superintendent's Cottage & Office

Daley Collection

shaft. A timbered tunnel 38 feet in length was built on the shore just above the high tide mark. It met the primary vertical shaft at 22 feet. The purposes for the tunnel were to assist in disposing of the rock and aid in ventilation.

By May 1882, the Faneuil Hall Mine had reached a depth of 165 feet with a cross cut being dug under the bay. They had been chasing a vein of silver for 350 feet. The vein of silver was 18 to 30 inches in width. In the same vein, a ton of ore produced a little over one ounce of gold! Things were looking up for the owners. But on the 20th of May, disaster came knocking. Superintendent Hayward's engineer Marcus M. Urann informed him that a large volume of water was seeping into the shaft near the silver vein. The water was reported to have come from a gravel vein that was near the silver. Miners previously had heard noises in the shaft that resembled rocks rolling on the drift's ceiling. The crosscut was at an incline in which the angle had made its way towards the bottom of the bay. Superintendent Hayward decided they had better investigate the water problem. Superintendent Hayward had Mr. Urann accompanied him on this investigation because he thought he may want to add an additional pump and would need Mr. Urann's assistance. Just as they were exiting the ore bucket at 165 feet, they heard a loud noise that sounded like water rushing and a strong wind hit them in the face. They realized that a massive wall of water was headed their way and that they may be killed if they could not exit the shaft in a timely manner. Superintendent Hayward rang the bell to let the hoist operator know that there was an emergency and they had to be raised immediately. The two of them were in a very desperate situation. The water in the shaft was rising faster than they were being hoisted. The bucket started to float and swing from side to side. The hoist operator realized they were in trouble. He panicked and throttled the engine to increase the speed of their ascent. He almost pulled the bucket through the gallows with them in it. This would have caused the gallows to collapse and the bucket to fall back into the shaft. The shaft depth being 165 feet is very similar to the height of Niagara

Falls. It was a long way to travel as they were being hoisted. It was reported one of the two stated his life was flashing in front of his eyes and he said he thought he was going to die. The standard ascent rate for a hoisting bucket was about a foot a second, but they were traveling faster. The water was filling the shaft and other drifts at a rapid rate. They escaped in the nick of time. They realized the rocks in this area that the miners had reported as being smooth had been tumbled by the ocean. The strong currents in the bay had rolled the rocks creating them to be smooth and this was the noise the miners heard above their heads.

The Faneuil Hall Mine was never reopened. It was determined that it would have been impossible to pump the shaft out. The water that came rushing in was saltwater from Taunton Bay. The company lost their pumps, pipes, air tanks, and anything else that belonged to the miners or company that was within the mine. Taunton Bay controlled the height of the water in the shaft. It would rise and fall at the same rate as the ebb and flow of the tide.

Jessie "Nannie" Daley's house was in close

proximity to the mine for it was on the north side of the graveyard directly across from the mine. John's father, Gerald Daley, as a young boy, would go there with his cousin Andrew Abbott and they would descend in the old shaft via ladders to the water level and would jump from the ladder to the tunnel. This tunnel would lead to the opening on the shore. The tunnel was blocked at the shore end with blasted rock that had been dumped there purposely to close off the shore entrance. Nannie

Faneuil Hall Mine Dump Pile Covers Opening on the Shore. Center, Old Wooden Piling from Wharf

Daley Collection

had told Gerald not to go near the mine for fear of him receiving an injury or drowning because he could not swim. John's father was a wonderful man, but not always well behaved. He told John he would play down by the mine for hours. A local storeowner, Eddie Crosby, plugged the vertical shaft in the 1950's. He feared children may be injured in a fall. He created a plug by covering the opening to the shaft with chicken fencing wire and

Looking Up Out of the Faneuil Hall Mine

Daley Collection

dumped loam onto the chicken wire. This created an earth plug. Today, when people clean Gordon Cemetery plots, they still toss old pots, leaves and plastic flowers into the area of the earth plug that resembles a divot in the ground.

Exploring the Faneuil Hall Mine

In 2003, John wanted to retrieve some of the old machinery to place on display. John and his father went down to the old shaft to investigate the possibility of making this happen. It was evident in order to obtain access to the vertical shaft, John would have to excavate manually about five to seven feet of grass, loam, and debris. John decided this was not a feasible idea for fear that once he opened the shaft it would leave a dangerous hole. He talked to Tomcat Gordon and asked him if he knew anything about the cave-in of the Faneuil Hall Mine. Tomcat was not aware of anything about the incident, nor if there was an opening to the shaft out in the bottom of the bay. Tomcat had lobster fished for over 60 years in Taunton Bay. He did say there was a shallow hole in the bay in front of the location of the Faneuil Hall Mine. He stated that if his lobster trap dropped into the hole, it caught a lot of lobsters. He did not believe the hole was there anymore because he was not able to find it over the past 30 years. He thought it had filled with sand that was being moved around by the current. Knowing that the cave-in took place about 350 feet from the shore, John thought there may be a hole in the bottom of the bay that would lead to the old Faneuil Hall Mine drift. Maybe, the hole Tomcat had located years earlier, was the opening that flooded the mine.

In the summer of 2011, during an Underwater Archeology Summer Field School, we decided we would try to find the opening. We needed to come up with a plan that would help locate the opening area, even if it had been filled with sand and/or gravel. We knew that the Faneuil Hall Mine was the only mine that had freshwater and a saltwater influx. Imagining what the spot would look like, we felt it would have limited plant life due to the fact that old-time fishermen would use freshwater to clean the marine life from the bottom of boats. It was reported that the height of the water in the shaft moved up and down with the tides, thus, transporting fresh water to the opening of the drift. Besides noticing a difference in marine life, we felt there would be a temperature change where the water would be coming out of the drift; it should be noticeably cooler. Ground water in the state of Maine is normally around 42 degrees. Bay water in mid-summer will be as high as 70 degrees.

On July 23, 2011, Keith and Kevin VanGorden, dive students; Padi Divemaster, Dean Smith and John went in search of the opening. Since the divers were identical twins, John made sure they wore different colored buoyancy compensator devices to assist with identifying the divers so the data from the dive would be accurately documented. Beyond the necessary dive gear the divers carried a thermometer. John's stepfather, Philip Stroup, would handle the boat while John was the designated safety/rescue diver. The group anchored the 20 foot *Corson* over the spot where John predicted the hole may have been. He estimated where the 350 foot spot from the shore would be; taking into account they were mining at an incline.

Faneuil Hall Mining Company

Even with all of our research, we were not sure what direction the crosscut went from the shaft. If it did not travel perpendicular to the shore, then they would not be anywhere near the cave-in. John decided a circular search pattern would be the most effective type of search to use. This would involve the divers tying off a 100 foot reel to the anchor line and making a circle pattern, extending it after each complete circle until the desired location is found. They would set the extended distance by the amount of visibility they had. The depth of the water was about 20 feet. The contour of the bottom was relatively flat, which allowed this pattern to be a great choice. A flat bottom would be necessary to prevent the line from entangling within any underwater obstructions, which would disrupt the divers circle. They agreed that Dean Smith would start the loop at the fifteen foot mark on the 100 foot reel. They set the distance between the divers after Dean reported that there was about 12 feet of visibility. It was decided that Keith would be set at the 30 foot mark and Kevin at the 45 foot mark. Kevin was to mark the bottom at the start with rocks

Faneuil Hall Mining Company

to let him know when he had made a complete circle. After making a full circle and not finding anything, the divers were to move out to the 60 foot mark. Kevin would go to the 60 foot mark, Keith to the 75 foot mark, and Dean to the 90 foot mark. If nothing was found, then they were to board the boat and John would reset the anchor and try again. John told the students that after this many years, he doubted there would be a noticeable hole. The water temperature on the bottom was 65 degrees. The students were to go slow and watch their thermometers. John recommended not wearing their neoprene gloves, so they would notice the temperature change easier with their bare hands. Also, they realized that there could be a problem if a freshwater spring naturally happened to be under the bay in the location they were looking. The water coming in and out of the Faneuil Hall mine would be brackish water and may be visible. The temperature should be a little warmer than 42 degrees yet colder than the 65 degree temperature of the bay water. Dean and the VanGordens were about halfway through their circle search when they

223

surfaced to report that they had found what they believed to be the area. Dean reported due to there being a temperature change and a large oval sandy shaped indention in the bottom he believed it was the Faneuil Hall Mine. The temperature on the bottom was around 53 degrees and no marine life was observed in this area. John suspected this to be the location where the water came in and out of the mine. From previous conversation with Tomcat, we believe this is the location he had described as the small hole in the bottom of the bay.

Dean brought up a trapezoid shaped bottle with raised letters that spelled "POISON." The blue bottle was about five inches tall, and had a cork stopper.

The Faneuil Hall Mine had a wharf that was positioned out in front of the mine. This is where they received their coal, other supplies and shipped their ore. John felt, that most likely any debris they would find, like the bottle, was not from the inside of the mine but garbage thrown overboard or from the wharf. It was a common practice to dispose of their refuse by throwing it into the ocean.

Sullivan Mining Company

The Sullivan Mining Company was built from two separate mines, the Sullivan Silver Mine and the Waukeag Silver Mine. The Sullivan Silver Mine was the first incorporated mine on the Sullivan Lode. In May of 1877, A. A. Messer discovered silver ore on the shore of Taunton Bay. The vein contained about ten inches of quartz and had traces of brittle silver. The vein ran below the high tide mark. A cofferdam was constructed to hold back the bay water. C. W. Kempton, a mining engineer, was hired to develop the mine. In 1878, the Sullivan Silver Mine was incorporated within the corporation laws of the State of Maine. The stock was offered at five dollars a share and up to 100,000 shares could be issued. The main corporate office was in the Tremont Bank Building, Boston, Massachusetts, in Office Number 17. George Brown was chosen as president and the other elected officers were F. R. Nourse as treasurer and W. Oscar Arnold as secretary. The corporate officers known as the directors were all from Boston. Their names were Joseph G. Russell, William D. Lewis, Lyman B. Greenleaf, and

Sullivan Mining Company

George G. Richards. The owners hired Mr. Thomas Cahill, formerly of the U.S. Mint at San Francisco, California, as the superintendent.

The Sullivan Silver Mine had 650 feet of linear measure on the Sullivan Lode. The mining works consisted of a Copeland & Bacon Steam Engine, which was located in the engine-house that was approximately 20 feet by 20 feet. The company had a large ore room, an assay office, and a business office. The first buildings on the grounds were quickly erected and not of high quality. The directors had been in a hurry to show some success and to help gather investors. A milling works would be built on site for the mine to process the ore. The main shaft was a traditional inclined shaft that ran 170 feet along the natural inclination of the ledge. A significant drift off from the main shaft was cut at the 65 foot level going east and west. The geologist, W. F. Stewart, wrote in his report that the vein at the second level of the Sullivan Silver Mine was three feet wide and up to ten feet in some sections. He stated that most of the silver was in a lead sulfide known as galena. Stewart estimated the value as high as several hundred dollars per ton of ore. Mr. Stewart felt when compared to the stocks of the silver mines of Nevada, the Sullivan Silver Mine Stock could be sold on the stock boards of San Francisco for a high sum of money.

In March of 1880, the Sullivan Silver Mine sold 2000 shares of stock at $14 a share designated to the construction of the bullion mill. They were able to construct the mill and have it operating by September of 1880, the first of its kind in the State of Maine. The mill started with 5 stamps, increased to 15 stamps and had plans for 30 stamps.

Special Correspondence of the Engineering and Mining Journal.

Last week, I visited the Sullivan District for the first time in eleven months. The mines there are looking finely.

The Sullivan has a stamp-mill, the first in the State, which is probably now in successful operation. It is a very substantial structure, and reflects credit on its builder and on the management of the mine. It was fitted with five stamps, but five more are to be added at once. One lot of bullion had been turned out previous to my visit, and the mill was at that time only awaiting the arrival of the iron chimney-cap to start up in earnest. The ore is first passed through a 10 X 7-inch Blake crusher; then through a drying-furnace: thence to the self-acting hopper that feeds the stamps. From the stamps an automatic screw apparatus carries it to an elevator, which takes it to the roasting and chloridizing furnace. It is then passed to the pans and amalgamators, near which are the retorts and smelting-furnace. Many hundred tons of ore are awaiting treatment, and the levels in the old shaft (incline) are in a condition to stope an immense amount in a short time. The incline is down 170 feet, with two levels, having some 600 feet of drifts in all. The vertical shaft is down 120 feet, and is provided with all appliances for working, having a Bacon hoisting-engine, Clayton compressor, Johnson drills, etc. Every thing about the premises does credit to the superintendent, Mr. B. P. Tilden, a great change being manifest since he took charge.

Courtesy Maine Mining Journal

Sullivan Mining Company

In 1879, approximately180 feet to the west of the Sullivan Silver Mine, the Waukeag Silver Mine started its operation. The Waukeag Silver Mine

(Along the shore L to R) Waukeag Mine Lifting Works, Tug
Phillip S. Eaton,
Sullivan Mine Lifting Works, and Sullivan Milling Works
Circa 1900

Courtesy Sullivan Sorrento Historical Society

owned 990 linear feet of the ore vein. It was incorporated with the same corporate guidelines as the Sullivan Silver Mine. Its corporate office was at the Sears Building in Boston, Massachusetts located in Room Number 4. The elected president was B. S. Grant from Boston. The other elected officers were W. Oscar Arnold as secretary and George E. Harrington as treasurer from Salem, Massachusetts.

Sullivan Mining Company

The remaining directors were C. H. Lewis and W. E. Connor of Brooklyn, New York and L. F. Morse, C. P. Weston, and G. G. Barker of Boston, Massachusetts.

Faneuil Hall Mine, Waukeag Mine, & Sullivan Mine
Circa 1880

Courtesy Maine Historic Preservation Commission.

The mine grounds consisted of a house for the gallows frame with hoisting works and engine room that was 25 feet by 40 feet and an ore house that was 36 feet by 100 feet. There was a building built for the miners' quarters. A small 25 horse power English steam engine was running the mining works. The main shaft had been driven to a depth of 70 feet. The ore was very consistent with the Sullivan Silver Mine's ore grade.

On March 18, 1881, the State of Maine approved the incorporation of the Sullivan Silver Mine and

Sullivan Mining Company

the Waukeag Silver Mine. They became known as the Sullivan Waukeag Mining Company with all interest and properties as one business. The new company could sell up to $1,000,000 in stock at five dollars a share. The first corporate officers were Joseph D. Prescott, Samuel L. Symonds, Gustavus S. Fernald, and John Shoenbar. It was their duty to organize the company and to elect by ballot the president, secretary, treasurer and its five or seven directors.

In May 1881, the stockholders of the Sullivan Waukeag Mining Company reorganized once again to be renamed the Sullivan Mining Company. At their shareholders' meeting held in Kittery, Maine, they chose to elect George B. Brown as president. F. R. Nourse as treasurer and the four directors were B. S. Grant, C. F. Farrington, Joseph G. Russell, and Dudley R. Child. The new company was allowed to issue stock certificates under its new corporate name. The newspaper, Boston Advertiser, wrote that this was an act of cooperate suicide. The law allowed for the stockholders only to be responsible for debt up to the proportion of

Sullivan Mining Company

their ownership. The Sullivan Mining Company took full advantage of this loophole in the law. The directors of the Sullivan Mining Company stated

Sullivan Mining Company

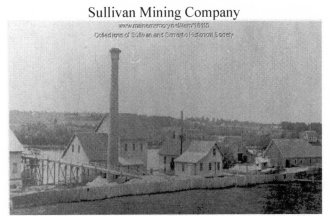

Courtesy Sullivan Sorrento Historical Society

that the newspaper would find the Sullivan Mining Company a very lively corpse. The Sullivan Mining Company reached a depth of 420 feet and had a total of nearly 2,204 feet of underground work. On February 17, 1883, the State of Maine authorized the Sullivan Mining Company to mine ore under the Sullivan River, Taunton Bay. This gave the Sullivan Mining Company the rights to excavate under the river below the line of low water mark. This was the length of the extension across the river perpendicular to the course of the river. It was to be directly in front of the mine's mining rights on the Sullivan side of Taunton Bay.

The mine had a constant problem with water. The directors decided to hire Mr. E. D. Leavitt Jr. an engineer with the Calumet & Hecla Mining Company to help solve the water problem. He installed two large Cornish Plunger Pumps; the first pump was placed at the 270 foot level to assist with pushing the water out of the mine along with the second pump that was placed at the bottom of the mine. They were 12 inches in diameter and had a six-foot stroke, which the water was forced up a ten inch pipe. With every stroke, a capacity of thirty gallons of water could be moved up the pipe. Thus, the pumps could pump about 300 gallons of water per minute. By using this process, the company was able to reduce their cost of pumping water by 75 percent.

The stamp mill was at best an experiment. It was designed after the smelters that were built out west. It worked poorly on the extremely hard rock of Sullivan. The stamp mill was always breaking down because of cold spots in the furnace. The furnace did not have enough tuyeres or air inlet holes. The mill had fans to assist in adding more air to the furnace, but they were not powerful enough. The mixture of crushed ore that was being smelted

Hard Rock Stamp Mill Similar Design to Sullivan Mine Stamp Mill

Courtesy California Historical Society

in the furnace would congeal and make a mess. The oven frequently needed to be torn down, cleaned, and rebuilt. This became the norm and was expensive.

The process of milling involved taking large chunks of ore to the crusher; after which, it passed to the stamps. Then, the ore was pulverized by the stamps so it could pass through a screen, which contained forty mesh holes per inch. The pulverized material was carried by an elevator to revolving, roasting, and chloridizing furnaces. The ore was cooked with common salt to create silver chloride, which took about 6 to 10 hours of roasting. The ore was put on the floor to be cooled. It was then placed in the amalgamating pans and mercury was added. This brought about a separation and the silver was put in settlers to be casted as bricks.

The Sullivan Mining Company closed in 1883 but was reopened several times after the price of silver rebounded. In 1884 to add insult to injury, the Sullivan Mining Company was taken to court. A year earlier, an independent contractor, Romana C. Mayhew, was hired by the company to trace veins of new ore. Mr. Mayhew descended to the 250 foot level of the mine and stepped out of the ore bucket. He planned to start looking for veins when, all of a sudden, about twenty inches away from the bucket, he fell through a 3 foot long by 26 inch wide unknown ladder hole. He claimed the mine Superintendent Cahill had ordered a worker by the last name of Stanley to cut a ladder hole and never warned him of this new hole. Stanley did not put up a protective rail or barrier. Mayhew fell 35 feet and seriously injured himself. He sued the Sullivan Mining Company for his suffering and injuries. The Sullivan Mining Company argued it was common not to have rails or barriers around ladder holes. The company wanted to have Mr. Stanley testify. They wanted him to be asked the question, if as a miner, was it practical or had he ever seen a rail or barrier around a ladder hole. The court would not allow for Mr. Stanley to be interviewed. The jury decided in the favor of Mr. Mayhew, and he was awarded $2,500. The court decided that a universal past practice for unsafe actions was not a basis for defense. The settlement was a financial burden for the mining company.

On September 1, 1885, the Sullivan Mining Company sold the land, buildings, wharf and all of its machinery to William B. Mason of Ellsworth, Maine. He purchased all of the rights from the company and even the stamp-mill machinery for the sum of $5,000. By 1910, the shafts were in desperate need of repair and the vertical shaft of the

Sullivan Mining Company

old Waukeag Mine was impassable. The milling works were sold to alleviate some of the debt. The Waukeag miners' quarters were later sold and the building was dragged by oxen from the shore to be placed next to the main road in North Sullivan. This building was again sold and renovated to be a store owned by Eddie and Dot Crosby. After that, it was owned by Jerry Turner and ran as a hardware store. The Sullivan miner's quarters was renovated and became known as The Granite Hotel. The original shaft house of the Sullivan Mine for the inclined shaft was renovated and Arthur Bunker operated it as the Sullivan Boarding House.

It has been long rumored that the remaining machinery was covered in cosmoline grease and placed in the incline shaft of the Sullivan Silver Mine. The opening of the shaft was then covered with the excess mining ore. The owner was always hoping to have the price of silver go up and have other investors become involved. During the years of its operation, it processed nearly 25 tons of silver lead bullion and was able to cast 310 pounds of silver. A bar of silver weighed about 47 pounds.

Exploring the Sullivan Mining Company

In the 1990's, we became interested in discovering what happened to all of the old machinery in the Sullivan Mine. John had an idea of recovering one of the old steam engines and repairing it to running condition. He wanted to exhibit the engine by having it on a trailer and displaying it in local festivities, such as the Sullivan Daze. John interviewed many of the local people who may have some knowledge about whatever happened to the equipment. We checked at the Sullivan Sorrento Historical Society for some leads into our investigation. We were provided with the names of people who might be able to assist us in our quest. John talked with Tomcat Gordon who, as a young man, had lived within a few hundred feet of the mine. He told John that his father had told him the equipment had been stored inside the incline shaft. When asked where the incline shaft was located, Tomcat said that it was behind the blocks of the steam engine mount. Another person John interviewed was Alan "Bussy" Dunbar, and he informed John that during the early 1960's that he could remember a giant steam engine flywheel laying on the mine's ore dump. Bussy believed at that time a junk metal dealer in the area retrieved it for scrap. Bussy felt the wheel was too tall to fit into the shaft, was removed from the steam engine and placed on the ore dump pile. John's father, Gerald Daley, who like Tomcat had grown up close to the mine, told him nearly the same story as Tomcat. He said that he thought it was behind the massive ore dump located behind Jerry Turner's Hardware. John later interviewed Prescott Briggs, Andrew Abbott, Frank Severance, Cecil Havey Jr., and Curt Davis. They all told similar stories with little variations. One of the similar stories most of the men agreed upon was that the inclined shaft was located in the basement of the old Sullivan Boarding House. The Sullivan Boarding House, originally was one of the Sullivan Mine's buildings, which had been renovated as a boarding house owned by Author Bunker. Nannie had worked at the boarding house as a young woman cooking for the bridge crew that built the Sullivan Bridge in 1926. John asked her about this story. She stated to him that she could remember an opening down in the cellar. She said she would place preserves in the opening because it was always cool. Her memory told her it had something to do with the mines.

We later gathered as much written material as we could to assist us in finding the opening of the incline shaft. At the Bangor Public Library in Bangor, Maine, we read selected sections of the *Maine Mining Journal*. It described where the three shafts were located on the Sullivan Mining Company property. We felt it was important to be able to uncover all of the identifiable features of the mines. The paperwork describes two vertical shafts and one incline shaft. The two vertical shafts were easy to find. The old Waukeag vertical shaft is located in front of Dr. Chris and Suzanne Mace's home near the shore. In the 1970's, Jerry Turner turned it into a bait well because the water never froze during the winter. The entrance to the shaft is

Sullivan Mining Company

filled with water, sand and debris. By digging on the side of the spring, we were able to find the old timbers of the shaft. The large granite blocks that are stacked and fastened together near this location was the base for the Waukeag steam engine. Iron

Originally the Steam Engine Base for the Waukeag Mine

Daley Collection

rods passed down through the granite blocks so vibration would not separate the blocks. A slanted cut was made in the blocks to allow for the fly wheel to turn. The other vertical shaft on the Sullivan Mining Company property is located in front of Hollis and Ellie Hills' house. It is in a small group of spruce trees near the shore. The old mill work's foundation where the stamp mill was located is about 30 feet in front of the Hills' home.

Remains of the foundation of the Sullivan Mine Stamp Mill

Daley Collection

The inclined shaft where the old machinery is supposedly stored was on the shore or in the basement of the Sullivan Boarding House. The *Maine Mining Journal* tells about a cofferdam being built to keep the tidewater from entering the shaft.

Marlene's, sister, Marilyn and her husband Robbie Reed showed an intense interest in our project and offered their assistance. Robbie was a foreman at Lincoln Pulp and Paper Mill and was experienced in using heavy equipment. He suggested we should rent an excavator and check out areas in an attempt to locate the incline shaft. We rented a backhoe and for nearly six hours, we dug test holes to obtain an idea of where the shafts

Sullivan Mining Company

and buildings were located. In the large ore dump pile in front of the Mace's house; we were able to find blasting wire and old drainpipes. We agreed this would be a good place for the incline shaft, since the stories included filling in the front of the shaft with ore in order to protect the machinery. We suspected this dump pile of ore may have been

Dump Pile for the Sullivan Mining Company

Daley Collection

used to close the shaft. Near the top of the dump pile, we uncovered old wooden beams, which we believed this to be the old shaft gallows that may have been discarded into the ore dump pile. We unearthed another area directly next to the stacked granite, which was where the Waukeag steam engine sat. We excavated six feet down in an attempt to find the bottom of the granite platform. We uncovered a large amount of coal ash and believed this was where the firebox to the boiler most likely sat. The contour of the land, in this area, had gone through many different changes in the last 100 years. We were not able to definitively locate the incline shaft. We know an opening to an air fluke going to the chimney was in the basement of the old boarding house. We wonder if what Nannie and others thought was the opening to the incline shaft may have been the opening to an air fluke. The flukes are underground; about three feet in diameter, bricked lined, and continue 100 feet back to the chimney. There are several other air flukes that can be found on the property. The foundation to the large chimney is on the Hills' home site. Our best guess for the location of the opening to the incline shaft is it lies between the two vertical shafts of the Waukeag Mine and the Sullivan Mine. It would have started on the shore

Sullivan Mining Company

in front of where the Sullivan Boarding House was located, due to the fact a cofferdam had been built around the opening. We were able to verify the sale of the milling equipment. Since we could not identify where the steam engines were sold, we believe the machinery still lies within the inclined shaft.

Most Likely the Drainpipe for the Sullivan Incline Shaft
Located on the Shore

Daley Collection

Milton Mining and Milling Company

The Milton Mining and Milling Company was incorporated in 1879, having a central office, in the Sears Building, in Office Number 4, Boston, Massachusetts. Joseph D. Prescott was elected as President. George E. Harrington, from Salem, Massachusetts, was elected treasurer. W. Oscar Arnold was elected secretary. The five directors were Joseph Prescott, L. Foster Morse, William D. Lewis, and Thomas Guernsey, all from Boston, Massachusetts. The Milton Mining and Milling

Milton Mine and Milling Works
Circa 1881

Courtesy of Maine Historic Preservation Commission

Milton Mining and Milling Company

Company, referred to as the Milton Mine, owned approximately 850 linear feet of ore channel. On February 17, 1883, the State of Maine passed legislation giving permission for the Milton Mine to mine under the Sullivan River, Taunton Bay. They had been doing so for over four years before given legal authorization. The owners hired Mr. John Shoenbar from out west as their superintendent. He had lived in California and Nevada and worked as the superintendent on the Pacific Coast for different gold and silver mines. He claimed to have been a colonel for the North during the Civil War. The owners hired C. L. Walker as the chief engineer. He had extensive experience working in the California and Nevada mines. He was formally employed by the Putnam Machine Works and had been in charge of the Burleigh Drills at the Hoosae Tunnel.

The Milton Mine offered 100,000 shares of stock at five dollars a share. With their investors' money, they constructed the largest and most extensive mining plant east of Comstock, Nevada, which included its own sawmill. The Milton Mine had extensive buildings, machinery, and had plans to included forty stamps. The largest building was called Shaft House No. 2. The building was 101 feet long and 32 feet wide. It had two full stories in one section of the building and was three stories in the other section. The difference in the heights was to allow for the height of the gallows frame. Inside this building were the gallows, machine shop, engine and boiler room, carpenter shop, foreman's

Gallows Frame Milton Mine
Circa 1880

Daley Collection-Published by C.L. Marston, Bangor, Maine

office, bathroom, and changing room with hot and cold running water for showers. There was 3,250 feet of iron pipe laid from a water source to the mine that had a head pressure of 60 feet of elevation. This provided an inexhaustible water supply for the entire mining complex. Water was accessible in all of the buildings. The availability of showers was used in advertisements as a draw to employ the over 50 men needed to operate the mine.

The Milton Mine had two shafts. The Shaft Number 2 was in Shaft House Number 2. Shaft Number 1 lays 185 feet east of Shaft Number 2 within Shaft House Number 1. There was a total of nearly 2,400 feet of underground drifts by 1883 from the two shafts. An underground crosscut connects the two shafts. Having two shafts helped with the air quality problem that most of the mines had. It also made it easier to have two above ground access points to move equipment, ore, and men. In Shaft Number 1, there was a crosscut at the 160 foot level that goes to the south nearly 400 feet under the bay. They cut numerous drifts to assist in getting closer to the vein. The miners would cut the drifts at an incline so the water would drain back to the sump of the mine. In Shaft Number 2 at the 180 foot level, they had a cross cut to the north for a distance of approximately 310 feet. In all, the Milton Mine has approximately a half mile of underground excavation.

The shafts had a double compartment with each compartment being four feet by four and a half feet. The compartment divide was made of timber and

Double Compartment Shaft of the Milton Silver & Milling Works Circa 1880

Daley Collection-Published by C.L. Marston, Bangor, Maine

went to a depth of 40 feet. At this point, the shaft became one compartment. The shaft was cribbed with massive timbers and iron fasteners all the way to the bottom. The wood materials came from the local area and were sawed at the Milton Mine Sawmill.

The archway below the gallows continued down to the bedrock. The archway was made from bricks, mortar and oak. The oak was designed in a half moon shape to support the brick arch. The amount of weight to be lifted by the gallows frame needed a solid base to prevent it from collapsing. The archway was beautifully constructed and has

Masonry Work of the Archway Below the Gallows in Shaft Number 2 Milton Mine

Daley Collection

lasted all these years. The gallows dimensions were 16 feet by 18 feet at the base, and it extended upward to 35 feet. A one inch diameter cable was used in the hoisting. A 50 horsepower Copeland & Bacon Steam Engine ran all of the machinery. A second steam engine was placed in operation by E. Hodge of East Boston. It was a 60 horsepower engine to supply power to the Burleigh Air Compressor. It had an air tank which measured 12 feet long by 51 inches in diameter. The compressor provided power to the three Burleigh Rock Drills and to the three Knowles Patent Steam Pumps used in excavating the mine. Water seeping into the shafts and drifts would flow back to the sump of the shaft and would fill the mine within a few days if it was not pumped out. This made it important to have the pumps operating continuously to stay ahead of the water flow. The Knowles Pumps were located in the sump of the shaft and were designed to push the water out of the shaft. The drainpipes used with the pumps were five inches in diameter. They were a spiral iron band encased with asbestos. They would attach the drainpipes to the shaft timbers to keep the drainpipes out of the way while using the shaft and to keep them in place while pumping the water out of the shafts.

Knowles' Patent Steam Pumps Ad

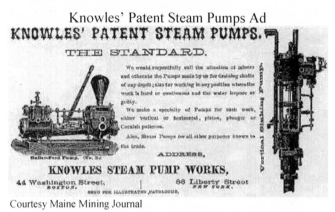

Courtesy Maine Mining Journal

A 15 horsepower Little Giant Steam Engine built by the Putnam Machine Company of Fitchburg, Massachusetts, supplied the power to the laths, circular saws and other machinery used in the carpenter shops. It provided power for the amalgamation pan, and an Alden Crusher and Pulverizer for sampling ore. The elevator used for hoisting and lowering tools and lumber received its power from the Little Giant as well.

The largest chimney ever built in Maine for mining purposes was constructed for the Milton Mine's milling works. The chimney was 80 feet tall consisting of double walls made of brick with a ten inch space between them. The inside wall had a clear opening of four feet in diameter. The construction of the chimney design was created to protect the inside bricks from cracking. When hot bricks came into contact with cold air, they will crack and fall apart. From the bottom of the chimney to the top of the chimney the smoke would rise and slowly cool. The height would keep the smoke high enough so not to interfere with the mining activity. The bottom of the chimney would be very hot due to the temperature needed to smelt the ore. The chimney stack sat upon a large circular granite base. A lantern was placed at the top of the stack to aid in navigation for shipping. It was

Granite Foundation for the Milton Mill Chimney

Daley Collection

Milton Mining and Milling Company

considered the first reference light signal for ships navigating from Frenchman's Bay to Taunton Bay. By 1910, the chimney for the Milton Mine had been removed.

Underground flukes were constructed from bricks ran from the base of the chimney to the shore. These flukes provided the air to assist in obtaining the needed temperature for the smelting process. The primary fuel for the milling works was coal, which was shipped in from Philadelphia, Pennsylvania.

Milton Mine
Circa 1910

Daley Collection—Eastern Illustrating Company Belfast, Maine

Shaft House Number 1 was constructed over Shaft Number 1 and was a two story framed house measuring 20 feet wide by 52 feet long. The hoisting works was also constructed and timbered

Milton Mining and Milling Company

on the bedrock similar to that of gallows in Shaft House Number 2. A 35 horsepower Kendall & Roberts Steam Engine powered the hoisting works. A pier was constructed off from Shaft Number 1, which led to a coal bin storage area. Local schooners such as the *Wigwam* were contracted to bring loads of coal from Philadelphia to the Milton Mine and the coal would be used to power the steam engines.

A blacksmith shop and an office building were separately constructed on the premises. The blacksmith shop was 20 feet by 36 feet and was built near Shaft Number 1. All the metal work was completed within the shop. Metal items used while constructing the mines, building and/or repairing equipment for use within the mines, made metal working in high demand for the area. Most of the larger mining companies, like the Milton Mine would have their own blacksmith shop to insure their needs were top priority. The office building held the business office, assay office, and apartments.

Superintendent John Shoenbar was an inventor.

Milton Mining and Milling Company

He developed a new kind of cage for hoisting cars and/or men as well as to assist with mine safety. The problem was that when blasting took place in the mine, it was common to destroy shaft timbers. This cage would be lowered before blasting and the cage would assist in supporting the timbers. Shoenbar's steel cage could also be balanced before ascending or descending to prevent swinging. This

Milton Mine Cage Designed by Shoenbar

Daley Collection- Published by C.L. Marston, Bangor, Maine

was a great improvement over the old cages because sometimes groves had to be cut into the timbers to prevent the old cages from doing damage while swinging. The cage was made so it could easily transport the carts and/or men within the shaft. The miners would line up the rails inside the cage to the rails in the mine or shaft house and roll the carts in and out of the cage. To make it easy in the shaft house, the cage would be lifted higher than the floor

Milton Silver Mine Rails Near Shaft Opening

Daley Collection-Published by C.L. Marston, Bangor, Maine

and planks would be set in place to allow for the cart to be pushed out of the cage. This made for a more efficient way of transporting ore out of the mine to be assessed whether it went to the processing pile due to having enriched ore or to the ore dump pile. The old style buckets had wheels attached to the bucket and the men would push the bucket to transport ore out of the mine as they rolled

Ore Bucket used in Hard Rock Mining

Courtesy Library of Congress

it along the rails. The buckets did not have as much capacity as the carts did. The shape and size of the cart made it easier for transportation of the ore.

Mr. Shoenbar also had designed a 12,000 gallon water tank built for the purpose of having a reservoir in case of a fire. He tried to use the water tank as part of a siphoning system, in which a pump

Milton Mining and Milling Company

would not be required to drain the mine. The water would be drawn up from a siphon pipe in the sump of the mine to fill the tank. This siphoning process did not work. Mr. Shoenbar was trying to create a perpetual motion machine and was not successful.

The mill was designed after the Nevada quartz crushing mills located on the Comstock Lode. They had an Excelsior Amalgamating Pan and Alden Crusher and Pulverizer for testing and sampling ores. They used an amalgamation process. The mill had five stamps and planned to expand to forty stamps. The mill processed ore for several of the neighboring mines as well. It ran on a 35 horsepower steam engine and was able to process five tons of ore a day.

Superintendent Shoenbar had extra duties and was chosen as the superintendent for the Copperopolis Mine, located in Hancock. Shoenbar later was involved as a director for the Sullivan Waukeag Mining Company for a very short period of time. He, also, was closely connected to the operation of the Golden Circle Mine on Seward's Island, known today as Treasure Island, in Sorrento,

Milton Mining and Milling Company

Maine. The Milton Milling Works smelted the first ore for the Golden Circle until the Golden Circle's mill works was finished in Portland, Maine. This was one of the only designated gold mines in the area with its primary resource being gold.

Colonel John Shoenbar wore many hats in the mining business and was the go-to man in the area. He had been in California during the gold rush where he learned to be a mining engineer. For most of his life, he lived in Nevada, California, Maine, and Alaska. The Colonel had trouble with his finances and was constantly being sued by his creditors.

He was the creator and editor of the local weekly paper known as *The Sullivan Bulletin,* with its first edition published on April 10, 1880. It had a circulation of about 700 papers. On the first edition's front page, it had a picture of a large rooster with words coming out of its mouth to announce it was going to be a weekly update paper. It contained stories about what was going on around town and what was happening in the mines. He did not want the paper to be political in anyway.

Milton Mining and Milling Company

Shoenbar found himself overwhelmed with the duties involved with editing the paper during the mining boom. Due to his time being in high demand for his duties with mining, he decided he could no longer continue as the editor of the *Sullivan Bulletin*. The directors of the Milton Mine placed John C. Winterbotham as the new editor. He became the editor on August 10, 1880. The paper was fairly successful as long as the mines were active. *The Sullivan Bulletin* discontinued on January 6, 1883. The paper was moved by Mr. Winterbotham and Mr. D. F. Brady to Ellsworth. They changed the paper to a democratic paper, called the *Hancock County Bulletin*. This paper only lasted for twenty-six weeks. At this point, they suspended it due to lack of circulation and advertisement sales.

From 1873 to 1881, Mr. Shoenbar was very aggressive in acquiring mining property in Nevada. He was able to purchase public land for mining purposes at five dollars an acre. He purchased three different parcels of land for a total of 150 acres. This practice was called "patenting." Shoenbar

Milton Mining and Milling Company

would later sell, lease, or leave the land purchases to his heirs. The mineral rights are still owned by the present day owners, not the public.

The Milton Mine was no longer in business by 1884. The shareholders of mine sold most the machinery to pay off their debts. The steam engines were sold to the Ellsworth Electric Company. The steam engines were used to run the generators which produced the electricity for the Ellsworth area.

On March 6, 1885, Mr. Shoenbar was one of the directors who formed the corporation known as the Long Pond Water Company. It had a gravity feed pipe coming down from Long Pond to supply water to the Waukeag section of Sullivan, known today as Sorrento, Maine. Today, the Long Pond Water Company is still in existence and supplies water to many of the Sorrento residents.

Mr. Shoenbar later moved to Ketchikan, Alaska, where he purchased the Laskawanna Gold Mine. He renamed it the Schoenbar Mine. He spelled the mine's name differently than his name. He would also spell his name as Shonbar at times. In 1899, he claimed to be 68 years old during the Alaska Census.

In 1965, the citizens named their new school after the road where the school was to be located. It was called Schoenbar Middle School. The road was named after the mine at the end of the trail way, the Schoenbar Mine.

Colonel John Shoenbar and Toby in Ketchikan, Alaska
(Circa 1905)

Courtesy Ketchikan Museums (Alaska)

Milton Mining and Milling Company

Mr. Shoenbar was a man whose character was questionable to say the least, yet he always seemed to land trusted and respectable positions. He had stated he was from different states and countries. He claimed he was born in the United States and his parents were from Germany or Russian depending upon where he lived. He lived in a German neighborhood when he lived in Boston. He and his wife, Mamie, died in Oakland, California, after World War I.

Investigating the Milton Mine

In 1995, Marlene and John, purchased Stuffy's Take-Out from a bank auction. It is located on part of the property of the Milton Mine and is now called The Galley Restaurant. This is predominately the area where the milling works, chimney, and a small section of Shaft House Number 2 were located. We noticed there were a lot of bricks on the shore and saw strange physical

Milton Mining and Milling Company

features on the land. There was a shallow depression in the back lawn near the fence that borders Robert "Robbie" Sumner's property. This captivated our interest to discover more about our property and about mining in Sullivan. We discussed our interest in the Milton Mine with Robbie. The Milton Mining and Milling Works Company encompassed Robbie's land and the land where The Galley Restaurant is situated. On Robbie's land, the rest of the Shaft House Number 2, Shaft House Number 1, the blacksmith shop, saw mill, business office and both mine shafts were located. Today, the buildings are long gone, but the foundation stones of some of the buildings can be found on the property. The shafts are still there, but full of clean, clear, fresh water. The foundation to the chimney is on the back lawn of The Galley Restaurant, which consists of large pieces of circular granite stones. Some of the bricks from the old chimney were sold after the closure of the mine while others lay on the shore. The openings to the chimney flukes are buried with tailings and loam. The brick lined fluke tunnels are still underground and lead from the shore to the base of the chimney. Some of the ore tailings lay beneath the lawn that was constructed around Robbie's house. Loam was brought in to cover the ore tailings and create a lawn. On the sides of the banks you can find ash piles where the coal ash from the mine's operations was dumped. Shaft Number 2, is now covered by a cement floor in the basement of Robbie's home. You would not know the shaft is there except there is a cut out plug in the floor, which allows access into the shaft. Shaft Number 1 lies uncovered near the shore about 185 feet east from Shaft Number 2.

Robbie told us that he was game for whatever we wanted to do on his land. John explained if he could check out a few places on his property, this would assist us in gathering information. John told him that if he would allow us to do some investigative research on his property, we could obtain a clearer picture of what was there and how it had been developed. John informed him we planned to drain the mine shafts and enter them, take a lot of pictures, and do a search for historical artifacts. He wished us good luck and asked us not to get killed.

The first time John remembered laying eyes on Robbie Sumner, John was ten years old. One summer day, John was playing basketball in his driveway on the Eastside Road in Sorrento. He heard a lot of hollering and laughing and saw two cars slowly coming down the road. The first car was a red 1961 Chevrolet Convertible. The top was down and a teenage boy with long blonde hair was driving it. He was facing backwards and driving with his rear end sitting on the steering wheel. He was hollering flirtatious remarks to a bunch of pretty girls who were following in an old blue car. They were giggling and waving to the young man, as he wooed them with his backward driving skills. Needless to say, this was quite impressive to a young boy. John went inside his dad's garage and told him what he had just witnessed and announced, "I want to grow up and be just like that guy!" Later to discover, that guy was Robbie Sumner.

We spent countless hours in the Bangor Public Library and were able to gather important information. We interviewed a lot of local people and found out as much about the Milton Mine and the property as we could. John interviewed Harry Plummer, a local surveyor, whom we had hired to do some surveying. We knew Harry had done some work years earlier on the neighboring properties. Harry told John a funny, scary story about his introduction to the Milton Mine. Harry was hired by Dot Crosby, a Sullivan Resident, to survey some land that bordered the property. Harry said he was pulling a survey tape across the area near the shore. He started up a small hill when to his surprise; he fell backwards through rotten boards into water, which later was identified as Shaft Number 1. He said, "What a shock!" It was a hot day, but the water was so cold. Harry scrambled out of the shaft

Shaft #1 Cofferdam 2017

Daley Collection

Milton Mining and Milling Company

When he got back onto solid ground, he looked down through the broken wood that had covered the hole. He saw his white cap floating on the water. He knew, this could have been a disaster because he was the only one that knew where he was working. Harry said, "Thank God, I knew how to swim, and the water in the shaft was all the way up to the top."

One of the things that made a strong impression was we found out that the mines' superintendents ordered a significant number of mining pants, blue or brown jeans. The Milton Mining Company would provide jeans for the miners when they were working. They kept these pants in the changing room where the miners would change clothes after working their eight hour shifts. The larger mines would provide the miners with pants to wear in the shafts to help in the recruiting of workers. The jeans had many purposes within the mines. Water was a constant problem in all of the mines. A lot of the pipes that were used by the pumps sprung leaks at the connective joints. The miners would use a pair of old jeans, reverse wrap each leg around the pipe and pull them tight. This would slow down a

Milton Mining and Milling Company

leak. Many times the pants were used to protect an air hose to a drill and were placed at corners or on sharp objects in the shaft. They were wrapped around the drill handles to help protect hands from developing blisters.

The denim that was utilized to make the jeans by the Levi Strauss Company of San Francisco, California, was produced at the Amoskeag Manufacturing Company in Manchester, New Hampshire. The first jeans ever produced were in 1873. What made them unique was the use of copper rivets being placed at points of stress and strain on the material, like the pocket corners and the base of the button fly. They quickly became popular with the miners because of their ruggedness.

In 2001, a pair of blue jeans went to auction on E-Bay. The experts believe they were made in 1885. The jeans were found in a Nevada abandoned mine. The Levi Strauss Company won the auction with the highest bid of $46,532. This is the highest amount ever paid for a pair of denim jeans. In 2009, a pair of jeans was found which dated back to

Milton Mining and Milling Company

1879. They were purchased for $40,000 however; they were insured for an estimated value of $150,000. We were amazed at the prices denim collectors were paying for old Levi Jeans. To date, any jeans that have been found were located in deserted mines in Colorado, Nevada, or California. We knew the Sullivan mines were mostly closed by 1884. If any jeans were in these mines, they would be older than 1885. We knew that the mines in Sullivan were full of fresh cold water and that fresh cold water acted as a preservative. If any jeans existed in the mines, there was a great chance that the jeans would be persevered in mint condition.

We came up with numerous plans on how to retrieve a pair if they existed. John's first thought was to get an underwater video camera that would withstand the water pressure at depths from 160 to 180 feet. We measured both shafts with a rope and a window weight. The shafts had different depths for each shaft. We found that the recorded measurement of the shafts given by the company was accurate. We did not have the money to put forward for such a significant investment as an underwater video camera. John found plans to build an underwater video housing on the internet. The material needed was relatively cheap and could be picked up at Home Depot. He bought a piece of ten inch PVC Pipe for the housing. Sunrise Glass in Ellsworth made a circular half inch Plexiglas Lens for the housing. He had to plumb on handles that would be used to hold the lead weights for stabilization and negative buoyance. He designed a sealing lid that screwed onto the back of the housing. He wrapped plumber's tape onto the threads and used a large adjustable wrench to tighten the lid. He mounted scuba diving lights onto the sides of the housing. The video camera had to be turned on before the cap was closed because there were no external knobs to run the camera controls. He had thought about adding some, but decided against it because this would have been the most likely location for a leak.

Gerald Daley, Aaron Gilpatrick, Marlene, and John chose a beautiful warm day in June for the first recording. We turned the camera on, placed it in the underwater case and lowered it to 120 feet for a

Milton Mining and Milling Company

test run. We did not dare to go all the way to 160 foot mark yet. We used lobster warp line to lower the camera into the shaft. We slowly lowered and raised it. We could not wait to watch the video recording. The video was excellent for the first twenty feet in capturing what was on the walls of the shaft. The problem began not from leaks as we suspected, but from condensation. The water in the shaft stayed at a constant 42 degrees and the camera, while running, produced heat which created condensation. The auto focus went wild trying to focus on the condensation and the video became blurred. Gerald said the best thing to do would be to use burnt toast inside the vacant spaces around the camera. He thought this would absorb the moisture inside the case. It worked! Our next problem was the threads of the cap leaked as the case was lowered and risen within the shaft. The case filled with water and ruined the camera. We reluctantly gave up on this idea.

We suspected the drainpipe that we had found in the dump pile of the Sullivan Mining Company would be the same type of drainpipe that was used in the Milton Mine. It was made with asbestos covering a spiral metal coil. We knew that the drainpipes would go to the sump of the mine. John said if he could somehow attach a line to a drainpipe, we could retrieve it. A pair of jeans may be attached to the pipe. John, once again, went to the internet and decided to purchase an iron bromine magnet, sometimes called an earth magnet. They are considered the strongest magnet made. A company in Massachusetts was selling them on E-Bay. They can be dangerous if they get anywhere near someone who has a pacemaker. We decided to purchase one that hopefully would be strong enough to fasten itself to the drainpipe and stay attached as it was lifted. It was mid-March when the magnet arrived. John tested the magnet to see how powerful it was. If the magnet was held within two feet of a five pound hammer, it would be drawn to the magnet. John placed the magnet on the bumper of his truck and it took at least 100 pounds of force to release it.

The water in the shaft does not freeze, so being in the middle of March, was of no concern to John when he wanted to test his theory. He talked Aaron Gilpatrick into going over to the mine and assisting him with his experiment. We have known Aaron for many years. John was first introduced to Aaron through Aaron's dad, Ivan, who was the Principal at Winter Harbor Grammar School when John taught there. Aaron took scuba diving classes from us, and he has remained a dear friend. He is currently a professional diver, licensed sea captain and is a music instructor. John has been able through the years to talk Aaron into some crazy adventures. Even though, it was about 30 degrees outside, Aaron agreed to help him lower and raise the magnet. Aaron openly stated this was entirely a crazy idea and like many of John's schemes, it had little chance for success. John decided to choose Shaft Number 1 to test his idea using the magnet due to its easy access. The shaft was plumb, but with such a long distance to lower the magnet, it would be difficult. His fear was that the magnet would become entangled around an old timber or become attached to a wall spike. John placed a wooden beam across the width of the shaft's opening and lowered the magnet in the middle of one of the double compartments. He previously marked the line to know how deep the magnet was as he lowered it. When the magnet reached the 160 foot level, it attached to something. John pulled but it would not budge. He asked Aaron to assist him with raising the magnet. It started moving again, but was getting heavier. When it was within sixty feet of the surface, Aaron said, "I can't believe one of your crazy ideas may have worked." John said, "Don't jinx us and just keep steady tension on the line." They were within fifteen feet of having the magnet to the top, when all of a sudden there was no tension on the line. They wailed, "Oh, Noooo!" John hauled up the last fifteen feet of line and to their surprise attached to the magnet was three feet of broken drainpipe. What is suspected to have happened is as they were pulling the drainpipe, it was attached to a longer piece of pipe, which broke off and sank.

John and Marlene decided that, after not obtaining a set of jeans using a magnet we would now try to drain the mine. We felt that after draining the mine, we would lower ourselves to the bottom, and search for the valuable Levi jeans and other historical artifacts. We needed to recruit more people with the hopes of having a greater chance for success. We recruited our brother-in-law, Robbie Reed, and his friend Glen Gagnon from Lincoln. We were able to have Mark Andrews of Sullivan agree that he would provide his wrecker once draining the shaft was successful. The wrecker had a winch cable that could reach to the bottom of the mine. John asked his father to assist us because he was mechanically inclined, excelled at analyzing situations and coming up with solutions.

It was decided that our best chance for success would be to attempt draining the mine during the summer. We chose the weekend after the Fourth of July in 2003 to execute our plan. We would start on a Friday night pumping the shaft and would pump through the night. Mark should be able to lower Robbie Reed and John into the shaft by noontime Saturday. We had worked out mathematically the pumping volume, but could only guess on the actual volume of the shafts and drifts as well as the amount of water seeping into the mines and drifts. H. E. Sargent Corporation agreed to provide us with a 4 inch pump, generator, and a lot of connective drainpipe. In case of a breakdown with the wench on the wrecker, a hand winch on an aluminum tri-frame was provided. Access was easiest at Shaft Number 1. We knew when pumping Shaft Number 1, we would actually be emptying both shafts at the same time because they were connected near the 160 foot level with a crosscut. Robbie Sumner gave us access to both shafts and told us to do what we

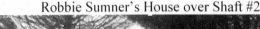

Robbie Sumner's House over Shaft #2

Daley Collection

needed to do to be successful. He said, if we needed to cut a larger hole in his basement floor to gain better access to Shaft Number 2, we could. It was good to know that Robbie Sumner supported the game plan. The current hole for access to Shaft Number 2 has a floor plug that is tapered and is about two feet by one foot in size. If we cut a larger hole, our concern would be making his basement floor more dangerous. John could visualize Robbie Sumner's daughter, Shaye, going down into their basement to get a can of corn and not coming up for supper. Through this hole, the archway and the bottom of the gallows can be seen.

Under the basement floor in Robert Sumner's House

Archway   and   Gallows

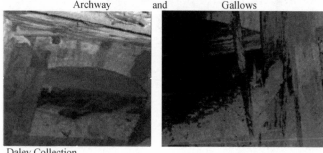

Daley Collection

We have been scuba instructors for many years and know that safety is built upon redundancy. We were not as concerned about entering the shaft as we were about exiting. What would we do if Mark's wrecker broke down? The aluminum tri-frame was not wide enough to go over the shaft, so as an immediate escape plan the hand winch and frame were out of the question. John had devised two other possible options to exit the shaft in case the wrecker failed to retrieve us. One was to deploy a skidder inner tube, fill it with air from a scuba tank, and shut off the drain pump. We would then sit on the tube and float to the top as the shaft filled with water. Before arriving at the surface, we would have to remain on the tube for about eighteen hours while the shaft filled. Based on our research, the mine would take about that long to fill. People could drop down supplies as needed. We would be wearing wetsuits to stay warm. John's second emergency option was to walk through the crosscut between Shaft Number 1 and Shaft Number 2. There was an old split rail wooden ladder in Shaft Number 2 attached to the wall that led to the top of the shaft. It had been submerged in fresh water for over one hundred twenty years, yet the ladder looked in decent condition. We could climb the ladder to the top of Shaft Number 2 in the basement of Robbie Sumner's house. We would have to have someone cut a larger hole in the basement so we could exit.

Milton Mining and Milling Company

We started the pump on that Friday at three o'clock in the afternoon. The pump had to be lowered into the shaft and would continue to descend as the water was pumped out. We would attach pipe extensions as needed. It worked marvelously! The pump weighed about 150 pounds

Shaft #1 (2 compartment) 4 inch Drain Pipe

Daley Collection

and could pump close to 500 gallons per minute. John tied the pump to the bumper of his Ford F-150 pickup. Our excitement over how well things were going should have been a precursor as to how terrible things could go.

Everyone went to bed around one in the morning, except for Robbie Reed and John. They kept fuel in the generator, which supplied the power to the pump. They also kept adding the 15 foot sections of pipe as they lowered the pump. At three in the morning, they had about the same amount of pipe in the shaft as they did on the ground. Robbie and John were standing near the shaft opening when all of a sudden Robbie asked, "Did you hear that?" John said, "Yes, it sounded like someone was throwing rocks at us." The pump was now at the depth of 60 feet inside the shaft. They ran over to

Shaft Number 2: Located Under Robert Sumner's House
(After Pumping Out 60 feet of Water)

Daley Collection

Robbie Sumner's basement to look down Shaft Number 2. As they suspected, the pump was taking the water out of both shafts at the same time. John was thinking that once the pump was at the 160 foot level, they would keep the pump going only as needed. They looked into the Shaft Number 2 and there were no obstructions in sight, it was a clear shot down the shaft. There was a split rail ladder still attached to the wall. Things were going great! They went back out to Shaft Number 1. Once again, they started hearing rocks being moved

Gerald Daley, Standing Next to Shaft Number 1

Daley Collection

around or thrown about. All of a sudden, the sixty feet of pipe that was lying on the ground began to move and squirm like a huge snake! It went plunging down the shaft! "Oh my God!" they exclaimed. They looked at each other as if to ask what caused that. The noise they were hearing was the gravel on the ground being pulled into the shaft with the pipe as the weight of the water filled pipe inside the shaft was greater than the weight of the water filled pipe outside the shaft. This weight was causing the pipe to be slowly dragged into the shaft. When the weight became too great, the rest of the pipe flew into the shaft. Thank goodness, the pump was tied to John's truck! They would have lost about a five thousand dollar pump into the mine. John started the truck and drove slowly forward lifting the pump out of the shaft. He was nervous about the strength of the rope used compared to the weight of the objects being lifted. He breathed a sigh of relief as Robbie informed him that the water was draining out of the pipe as the pump was being lifted. By slowly moving the truck forward, this allowed the water to have time to drain from the pipe. They were able to get everything out of the shaft safely. Robbie and John stood there with a sigh of relief. They discussed how lucky they were to have raised the pump safely. All of a sudden, a loud noise came from inside of Robbie Sumner's house from Shaft Number 2. They ran back to the basement to find out what caused such a commotion. To their amazement, when they looked down the shaft, they discovered the ladder which had been attached to the wall inside the shaft had fallen sixty feet into the water and possibly to the bottom of the shaft. Even though the wood of the

View Looking Down Through the Cutout in Shaft Number 2
(After the ladder had fallen that was attached to the iron wall brackets)

Daley Collection

ladder looked to be in great shape, it had been attached to the wall with iron brackets. The brackets had rusted and the weight of the water soaked ladder, without the support of the water in the shaft, was too great for the brackets to support. Robbie stated, "John, what would have happened to us if we had tried to use that ladder for an escape? We would have been most likely killed or severely injured with little chance of rescue." This concluded their attempt at reaching the bottom of the mine for the night.

In the morning during breakfast, we discussed the events of the night before. Marlene was convinced that the two of us could dive the mine and reach the bottom if we drained sixty feet of water out of the shaft. We have been trained in many different specialties, but neither of us have taken cave diving. The closest specialty our certification covers is overhead obstruction wreck diving. Overhead obstruction diving can be very dangerous. Diving in a mine is considered cave diving once you enter drifts. Marlene argued that this was not cave diving or overhead obstruction diving until we enter a drift. We knew that the crosscuts were constructed at an inclined angle. After you enter a crosscut, you should be able to swim your way toward the ending of the inclines where the water would not be able to fill the inclines due to the trapped air pockets. If you were able to breathe the air in the incline it is still compressed air. The deepest depth for diving on regular air is 130 feet. The problem is that you have limited bottom time before decompression will be required. The maximum allowable bottom time for a dive to 130 feet is 15 minutes without decompression stops. If you do not obey the rules, you can develop decompression illness, also known as the bends. Your body for some unknown reason while under pressure stores nitrogen in a liquid state and when the pressure is relieved, such as going to the surface, the nitrogen turns to gas. These bubbles will cause obstructions in the blood stream and severe pain in joints. Severe cases can cause paralysis or even death. The only treatment is to go to a recompression chamber, which is expensive and the closest chamber is at Saint Joseph Hospital in Bangor, Maine. You do not want to go beyond your no decompression limits if avoidable. You must do staged decompression stops if you surpass your no decompression limit. This would involve leaving scuba tanks on a down line for decompression stops. To complete the dive safely, not only is there the concern for decompression illness, but there are the concerns of nitrogen narcosis, visibility, limited room, condition of the shaft and its contents. John told Marlene, he was not sure what the condition of the bottom of the shaft would be after the attempt of lifting the pipe with the magnet. He was afraid that the falling pipe had created an entangled mess. Previously, John had, also, had a bad experience while diving in the Pine Tree Mine's shaft. He decided that the unknown risk outweighed the possible unknown gains.

Early Sunday morning, the shafts were full of water again. Oddly, an 1883 bottle of Coca/Wine was floating in Shaft Number 2. John used a smelt net to retrieve it from the shaft. The cork was still in it and the bottle contained about one third of its contents. He pulled the cork and what a foul odor the contents of 125 year old Coca Wine made! Now, we know what some of the miners were drinking on their last shift at the Milton mine.

Von Hauff's Coca Wine and Malt

Daley Collection

In 2011, we decided to dive where we perceived the location of the old pier to be next to Shaft Number 1. John took the University of Maine at Machias Underwater Archaeology students Keith and Kevin VanGordon and Divemaster Harry Fish to investigate this location. At low tide, we anchored the boat directly off from Shaft Number 1, in about 12 feet of water. The divers discovered

Milton Mining and Milling Company

one 40 foot rail, which resembled a rail from a railroad line. It was at an inclined angle with blocks underneath it going from a 12 foot depth of water up to about 6 feet towards the shore. Flat granite stones were used for the blocking. There were a lot of old bottles, broken glass, and some pieces of rusted iron throughout the area. Harry Fish felt the keels of the schooners rested on the rails due to this being the area where the schooners would unload and load their cargo such as coal and ore. A lot of times, other mines would send their ore to be processed at the Milton Mine.

We believe it is possible with the right crew, proper equipment, and a good plan to reach the bottom of the Milton Mine. Our hopes of reaching the bottom of the Milton Mine are not laid to rest as of yet. With further training, we eventually plan to have another attempt at successfully meeting our goal.

In March of 2017, we were able to lower a light system with a GoPro attached and take video of Shaft Number 1 to the 160 foot depth. The video showed numerous ladders at different levels within the shaft. On April 2, 2017, we invited Marilyn and Robbie Reed to help us attempt to obtain one of the ladders by lowering a grapple hook. Amazingly in twenty minutes, John was able to bring up a 11 foot split rail ladder. He hooked it at about the 70 foot level in the shaft. The ladder's rails were made out of pine and the rungs were made out of oak.

Two weeks later, Marlene and John were trying to retrieve another ladder that was seen in the video with the grapple hook. Marlene was able to hook something and brought it to the bottom of the double divided compartment. We could not budge it from there, so we left and came back the next day. Marlene was able to hook it again and with John's assistance was able to retrieve it. It was another ladder but this time it was a 20 foot long ladder! The water soaked ladder was so heavy, we asked Dylan Porter, a Maine Maritime Student, for assistance with carrying the ladder to The Galley.

We hope to dive the Milton Mine at a later date to the 160 foot level. We are very curious as to what lies within the mine. We are in hopes of retrieving more of the split rail ladders and maybe

Milton Mining and Milling Company

even a pair of Levi Jeans!

John and Marlene with the Ladders
May 30, 2017

Daley Collection

Epilogue

Many of the items recovered from our adventures are on display at the Sullivan Sorrento Historical Society, Hancock Historical Society and at The Galley Restaurant by the Hancock Sullivan Bridge. We continue to research the area's history, explore the sites, and teach Underwater Archeology classes at the University of Maine at Machias. We will continue to unearth and amass more of the local history for all to enjoy.

Bibliography

Sullivan Harbor and Sullivan Falls

Alexandria Gazette. (Alexandria, Virginia). "Poisoned by Impure Water." July 15, 1899.

Altoona Tribune. (Altoona, Pennsylvania). *"Captain and Crew Saved."* Pg. 1. August 25,1893.

American Lloyd's Register of American and Foreign Shipping. "Schooner *Julia S. Bailey."* Pg. 34. 1895.

American Lloyd's Register of American and Foreign Shipping. *"Schooner Maine."* Pg. 134. 1877.

American Lloyd's Register of American and Foreign Shipping. *"Schooner Wild Rover."* Pg. 314. 1885.

American Lloyd's Register of American and Foreign Shipping, 1868.*"Schooner Ganges."* Pg. 572. 1868.

American Lloyd's Register of American and Foreign Shipping, 1899. *"Schooner Lucy Belle."* Pg. 37. 1899.

American Lloyd's Register of American and Foreign Shipping, 1899. *"Schooner Franconia."* Pg. 39. 1899.

American Lloyd's Register of American and Foreign Shipping, 1868. *"Schooner Wide World."* Pg. 63. 1868.

American Lloyd's Register of American and Foreign Shipping, 1868. *"Schooner Alice R."* Pg. 13. 1868.

American Lloyd's Register of American and Foreign Shipping, 1867. *"Schooner Oregon."* Pg. 5. 1867.

Bangor Daily Whig and Courier. (Bangor, Maine). *"Hancock."* Pg.1. July 20, 1888.

Bangor Daily Whig and Courier. (Bangor, Maine). *"Sullivan Harbor Land Company."* Pg. 3. February 3, 1889.

Bangor Daily Whig and Courier. (Bangor, Maine). *"Hancock County."* March 28, 1891.

Bangor Daily Whig and Courier. (Bangor, Maine). *"From Ellsworth: The Ice in Frenchman's Bay."* Pg. 3. January 25, 1888.

Bangor Daily Whig and Courier. (Bangor, Maine). *"Disasters."* Pg. 3. November 19,1878.

Bangor Daily Whig and Courier. (Bangor, Maine). *"Sullivan Steam and Ferry Company."* Pg. 3. February 9, 1881.

Bibliography

Boston Herald. (Boston, Massachusetts). *"Ellsworth."* Pg. 5. November 17, 1910.

Boston Post. (Boston, Massachusetts). *"Sullivan Harbor Land Company."* Pg. 6. January 8, 1891.

Boston Post. (Boston, Massachusetts). *"Sullivan Harbor Land Company."* Pg. 6. February 20, 1891.

Boston Post. (Boston, Massachusetts). *"Sullivan Harbor Land Company."* Pg. 6. July 31, 1889.

Boston Post. (Boston, Massachusetts). *"Sullivan Harbor Land Company."* Pg. 5. February 20, 1891.

Boston Post. (Boston, Massachusetts). *"Burglars."* Pg. 2. April 22, 1876.

Boston Post. (Boston, Massachusetts). *"Mariner News."* Pg. 5. July 17, 1895.

Boston Post. (Boston, Massachusetts). "Lucy Belle Sunk Off Hatcher's.*"* Pg. 7. November 30, 1901.

Daily Eastern Argus. (Portland, Maine). *"Disasters."* Pg. 3. May 13, 1868.

Daily Eastern Argus. (Portland, Maine). *"Disasters."* Pg. 2. November 21, 1868.

Emerson, Kendall Benjamin and Joseph Hartshorn. "The Green Schists and Associated Granites and Porphyries of Rhode Island." US Government Print Office. 1907.
Evening Post. (New York, New York). *"State of Maine."* Pg. 1. August 30, 1838.

Fort Wayne Sentinel. (Fort Wayne, Indiana). *"Abandoned Schooner."* Pg. 1. April 13, 1894.

Galveston Daily News. (Galveston, Texas). *"A Big Society Stir."* Pg. 13. July 26, 1891.

Galveston Daily News. (Galveston, Texas). *"Maritime Notes."* Pg. 1. November 23, 1911.

Gardner, Arthur, H. *"Wrecks around Nantucket."* Publisher, Inquirer and Mirror Press. Pg. 106.

Honolulu Republican. (Honolulu, Hawaii). *"Will Not Build a Seven-Master."* Pg. 2. March 29, 1901.

Hopewell Herald. (Hopewell, New Jersey). *"Maine Was Painted Red By Prehistoric Indians."* Pg. 1. May 17, 1939.

Bibliography

Hull, Arthur M. and Sydney A. Hale. *"Coal Men of America: A Biographical and Historical Review."* Publisher, Chicago, The Retail Coalman. Pg. 225.

Moorehead, Warren King. (Augusta, Maine). *"A Report on the Archaeology of Maine: Sullivan Falls Cemetery."* Pg. 76. Published by State of Maine, 1922.

National Republican. (Washington, District of Columbia). *"Proposals: United States Engineer Office."* Pg. 3. April 7, 1874.
National Republican. (Washington, District of Columbia). *"Sullivan Falls Maine."* Pg. 1. November 3, 1874.

New York Herald. (New York, New York). *"Mariner News."* Pg. 10. August 3, 1895.

New York Times. (New York, New York). *"Gen. Sherman Also There- A Dinner to Cardinal Gibbons."* August 7, 1890.

New York Times. (New York, New York). *"Sullivan Harbor."* Pg. 5. August 4, 1895.

Ottawa Journal. (Ottawa, Ontario, Canada). *"Stevenson at Sorrento."* Pg. 6. August 9, 1894.

Philadelphia Inquirer. (Philadelphia, Pennsylvania). *"Schooner Lucy Bell Ashore."* Pg. 5. April 1, 1900.

Pittsburg Dispatch. (Pittsburg, Pennsylvania). *"Sullivan Harbor Land Company."* Pg. 1. July 19, 1891.

Pittsburg Dispatch. (Pittsburgh, Pennsylvania). *"A Big Society Stir."* Pg. 1. July 19, 1891.

Portsmouth Herald. (Portsmouth, New Hampshire). *"Red Paint People."* Pg. 4. September 27, 1940.

Portland Daily Press. (Portland, Maine). *"Matters in Maine."* Pg. 3. July 8, 1875.

Portland Daily Press. (Portland, Maine). *"Sullivan Falls."* Pg. 4. August 12, 1853.

Tri-Weekly Era. (Raleigh, North Carolina). *"Sullivan Falls."* September 5, 1872.

US Army Corps of Engineers. *"New England District: Sullivan Falls Harbor."* Published by USA. Government.

U.S. Gov. *"Report of the Chief of Engineers U.S. Army, Part 1."* Published by United States, Army, Corps of Engineers. Pg. 123. 1911.

Bibliography

Wichita Eagle. (Wichita, Kansas). *"Paul Dudley Sargent."* Pg. 1. November 8, 1883.

Taunton Bay Crossing

Annual Report: Maine Highway Commission. *"Sullivan and Hancock,"* Possible Bridge Construction. Pg. 197. December 21, 1916.

Bangor Daily Whig and Courier (Bangor, Maine). *"Sullivan Ferry."* December 24, 1987.

Bar Harbor Times. *"Property of Waukeag Ferry."* September 22, 1926.

Boston Advertisement, *"Paul Dudley Sargent."* Nevada State Journal (Reno, Nevada) November 7, 1883.

Maine Automobile Association. *"Maine Automobile Road Book."* Pg. 246. 1914.

Maine Gov. *"Special Laws of the State of Maine Passed by the Legislature."* Published by Maine State Government. Pg. 64. March 8, 1821.

Maine Gov. *"Special Laws of the State of Maine Passed by the Legislature."* Published by Maine State Government. Pg. 293. February 8, 1823.

Maine Gov. *"Private and Special Laws of the State of Maine from 1875, Inclusive."* Published by Maine State Government. Pg. 9. 1875.

Maine Gov. *"Public Documents of the State of Maine: Being the Reports of the State Of Maine 1916."* Published by Maine State Government pg. 197. December 20, 1916.

Maine Gov. *"Acts and Resolves as Passed by the Maine Legislature."* Published by Maine State Government. Pg. 390. June 19, 1846.

Maine Gov. *"Acts and Resolves as Passed by the Maine Legislature."* Published by Maine State Government. Pg. 475. April 5, 1921.

Maine Gov. *"Acts and Resolves as Passed by the Maine Legislature."* Published by Maine State Government. Pg. 470. April 1, 1919.

Maine Gov. *"Acts and Resolves as Passed by the Maine Legislature."* Published by Maine State Government. Pg. 203. February 8, 1867.

Maine Supreme Judicial Court. *"Waukeag Ferry v. Hancock County Commissioners."* Published by Supreme Judicial Court of Maine, Hancock County. April 11, 1929.

New York Tribune (New York, New York) *"Instances Related Where an Attempt to Exercise This Power Proved of Doubtful Benefit."* September 17, 1911.

Bibliography

Shaw, Richard R. *"Around Blue Hill and Ellsworth."* Published by Arcadia Publishing. Pg. 17. 2008.

The Automobile Blue Book. Volume 2. 1917.

Crabtree Ledge Lighthouse

American Engineer- Volume 15-16. *"Lighthouses."* Pg. 224. December 19, 1888.

Bangor Daily Whig and Courier. (Bangor, Maine). *"Hancock."* Pg. 4. December 8, 1894.

Bangor Daily Whig and Courier. (Bangor, Maine). *"Hancock."* Pg.1. January 7, 1893.

Bangor Daily Whig and Courier. (Bangor, Maine). *"Sebenoa."* Pg. 3. February 13, 1893.

Bangor Daily Whig and Courier. (Bangor, Maine). *"Bar Harbor News."* Pg. 4. August 18, 1896.

Bangor Daily Whig and Courier. (Bangor, Maine). *"Sebenoa Saved Sullivan."* Pg. 2. February 3, 1898.

Bangor Daily Whig and Courier. (Bangor, Maine). *"Hancock."* Pg. 3. October 1, 1896.

Bangor Daily Whig and Courier. (Bangor, Maine). *"Sebenoa."* Pg.4. November 7, 1895.

Bar Harbor Times. *"Sebenoa."* July 22, 1903.

Bar Harbor Times. "Tragedy at Hancock Point." October 7, 1916.

Bar Harbor Record. *"Sebenoa Wrecked."* November 23, 1898.

Boston Post. (Boston, Massachusetts). *"Harbor News."* Pg. 9. June 1, 1901.

Chicago Daily Tribune. (Chicago, Illinois). *"Cleveland Will Go to Sorrento."* Pg. 6. July 22, 1892.

D'Entremont, Jeremy. *"The Lighthouses of Maine."* Commonwealth Edition. June 1, 2009.

Eaton, Aurore. New Hampshire Union Leader. *"Looking Back."* December 18, 2014.

Greene, Francis B. *"History of Boothbay, Southport Boothbay Harbor."* Maine Historical Society. Pg. 420. 1905.

Bibliography

Lebanon Daily News. (Lebanon, Pennsylvania). *"A Rum Jug at the Masthead."* Pg. 1. October 28, 1889.

Lighthouse Inspection Reports Database, Crabtree Ledge Light Station. Premises pg. 2.

Marine Review. Volume 30 Pg. 35. 1904.

Mount Desert Herald. *"Steamer Sebenoa."* March 23 1888.

Oakland Tribune. (Oakland, California). *"Sebenoa."* pg. 5. July 20, 1895.

Register: American Lloyd's Register of American and Foreign Shipping, *"Vessel: Cape Ann."* Master: Greenlow.1861.

The Bridgeport Telegram. (Bridgeport Connecticut). *"Harbor News."* Pg.9. June 22, 1922.

The Daily Gazette. (Fort Wayne, Indiana). *"Death or Injury."* Pg. 6. August 6, 1884.

Trapani, Bob Jr. *"Shadow of Death Follows Crabtree Ledge Lighthouse to a Watery Grave."* Lighthouse Digest. Published November 2005.

United States Department of Commerce and Labor. *"Reports of the Department of Commerce and Labor."* Pg. 365. 1904.

Schooner Mabel Goss

Annual Report of the Operations of the United States Life-saving Service. *"British Schooner Lizzie B."* Pg. 112. October 12, 1894.

Annual Report of the Operations of the United States. *"Life-Saving Service 1896."* Washington: Government Printing Office. Pg. 48. 1896.

Boston Post. (Boston, Massachusetts). *"Water Front."* Pg. 3. October 14, 1897.

Daley, John and Marlene. *"Schooner Mabel E. Goss Shipwreck Survey."* University of Maine at Machias. Report submitted to the Maine Historic Preservation Commission, Augusta, Maine. 2003.

Grenon, Ingrid. *"Down East Schooners and Shipmasters."* Published by History Press, Charleston, SC 2012.

Leavitt, John F. *"Wake of the Coasters."* Published by Maritime Historical Association, by Wesleyan University Press, Pg. 152. October 22, 1970.

MacKinnon, Robert and Dallas Murphy. *"Treasurer Hunter: Diving for Gold on North America's Death Coast."* Published by the Berkley Publishing Group, New York, New York, 2012.
Marine Journal, *"Annual List of Merchant Vessels of the United States."*

Bibliography

Volume 43. Shipbuilding 1921.

National Archives Project. *"Ship Registers and Enrollments of Machias, Maine, 1780-1930."* Pg. 155.

Sessional Papers of the Dominion of Canada. *"Sessional Papers, Schooner Lizzie B."* Sessional Papers. Vol. 40. Issue 9. Pg. 270.

Torrey, Fred A. *"Special Collections: Guide to the John L. Goss-Papers."* Raymond H. Folger Library, Special Collections Department. January 2005.

Schooner Abbie Bursley

American Lloyd's Register of American and Foreign Shipping 1865-1895. *"Schooner Bursley."*

American Lloyd's Register of American and Foreign Shipping 1883. *"Key to Abbreviations."* Pg. 23 of 31.

Annual Report 1880. Published by United States Army Signal Corps. "February 3, 1880. Pg. 86.

Annual Report 1880. Published by United States Life-Saving Service for the Years 1880. Pg. 106.

Brooklyn Daily Eagle. (Brooklyn, New York). *"Two Collisions."* Pg. 4. December 7, 1885.

Coogan, Jim. *"Sea Takes a Toll On Cape Family."* Published by Summerscape, June 25, 2010.

Eastman, Shirley. *"Osterville."* Arcadia Publishing, pg. 14. 2010.

Grenon, Ingrid. *"Down East Schooners and Shipmasters."* Published by History Press, Charleston, SC 2012.

Miller, Stauffer. *"Cape Cod and the Civil War: The Raised Right Arm."* Published by History Press, Charleston, SC Pg. 51. 2010.

Phillips Library Digital Collection. Peabody Essex Museum. *"Burnham Family Papers."* Abbie Bursley, Identifier, MH51. 1805-1957.

Seamen's Friend. *"Singular Coincidence, An Entire Family Drowned."* Volume 42. Pg. 15. 1870.

Wilmington Morning Star. (Wilmington, North Carolina). *"Marine Notes."* Pg. 4. May 25, 1872.

Schooner William Gillum

American Lloyd's Register of American and Foreign Shipping 1881. *"Schooner William Gillum."* Page 162. 1881.

Bibliography

American Lloyd's Register of American and Foreign Shipping 1892. *"Schooner William Gillum."* Pg. 911. 1892.

District Court, D. Massachusetts. (Lowell, Massachusetts). *"General Average-Jettison of Deck Cargo-Libel, Against Vessel."* Case No. 17,693. September 1872.

Grenon, Ingrid. *"Down East Schooners and Shipmasters."* Published by History Press, Charleston, SC 2012.

Lowell, John. *"Judgments Delivered in the Courts of the United States for the District Lowell, Massachusetts."* Volume 2. Pg. 154. 1872.

MacKinnon, Robert and Dallas Murphy. *"Treasurer Hunter: Diving for Gold on North America's Death Coast."* Published by the Berkley Publishing Group, New York, New York, 2012.

Mining the Sullivan Lode

Interview. *"Andrew Abbott."* Sorrento, Maine. June 1994.

Interview. *"Cecil Havey."* Sullivan, Maine. June 1994.

Interview. *"Cecil Havey Jr."* Hancock, Maine. June 1994.

Interview. *"Curt Davis."* Sullivan, Maine. July 1996.

Interview. *"Irving Severance."* Sullivan, Maine. June1994.
Interview. *"Prescott Briggs II."* Sorrento, Maine. June 1994.

Interview. *"Woodrow Thompson."* Maine State Geologist. Sullivan, Maine. May 1998.

Kempton, C.W. *"Sketches of The New Mining District At Sullivan, Maine."* Mining Engineer, West Sullivan, Maine. March, 1880.

Leiner, Danielle. *"History of Three Silver Booms."* Metallix Company. Greenville, North Carolina. Posted on the Web. January 7, 2013.

Maine Mining Journal. *"Mining Sullivan District."* Published 28 West Market Square, Bangor, Maine 1880-1883.

Philbrick, F.C. *"Economic Geology Papers."* F.C. Philbrick & Co. Stationers, 101 Devonshire, 25 Water Street, Boston. 1904.

United States Geological Survey. *"Some Ore Deposits in Maine."* Bulletin 432, Department of The Interior. 1910.

Pine Tree Silver Mining Company

Edward G. Longacre. *"Corse, John Murray";*

Bibliography

http://www.anb.org/articles/04/04-00268.html

Kempton, C.W. *"Sketches of The New Mining District At Sullivan, Maine."* Mining Engineer, West Sullivan, Maine. March, 1880.
Maine Mining Journal. *"Pine Tree Silver Mine."* Published 28 West Market Square, Bangor, Maine 1880-1883.

National Speleological Society, Cave Diving Section P.O. Box 950 Branford, Florida 32006-0950

Faneuil Hall Mine

Maine Mining Journal. *"Faneuil Hall Mine."* Published 28 West Market Square, Bangor, Maine 1880-1883.

Ellsworth American. *"Sullivan Mine Cave In."* May 20, 1882.

New York Tribune. *"Silver in Maine."* August 27, 1879.

Interview. *"Jessie Daley."* Sullivan, Maine. June 1994.

Interview. *"Dorothy Crosby."* Sullivan, Maine. September 1992.

Interview. *"Gerald Daley."* Sullivan, Maine. June 2003.

Kempton, C.W. *"Sketches of The New Mining District At Sullivan, Maine."* Mining Engineer, West Sullivan, Maine. March, 1880.

Philbrick, F.C. *"Economic Geology Papers."* F.C. Philbrick & Co. Stationers, 101 Devonshire, 25 Water Street, Boston. 1904.

Underwater Archaeology Notes. *"Summer Field School 2011."* University of Maine at Machias, July 2011.

Sullivan Mining Company

Interview. *"Alan Dunbar."* Sullivan, Maine. May 1987.

Kempton, C.W. *"Sketches of The New Mining District At Sullivan, Maine."* Mining Engineer, West Sullivan, Maine. March, 1880.

Maine Mining Journal. *"Sullivan Waukeag Mining Company."* Published 28 West Market Square, Bangor, Maine 1880-1883.

Philbrick, F.C. *"Economic Geology Papers."* F.C. Philbrick & Co. Stationers, 101 Devonshire, 25 Water Street, Boston. 1904

Stewart, W.F. *"Economic Geology. Collected Papers, Volume 6."* West Sullivan, Maine. April 12, 1881.

Supreme Judicial Court of Maine. *"Mayhew V. Sullivan Mining Company."* Hancock County, Maine. April 5, 1884.

Bibliography

Underwater Archaeology Notes. *"Summer Field School 2011."* University of Maine at Machias, July 2011.

Milton Mining and Milling Company

Allen, June. *"Name It Schoenbar: What's in a Name?"* Stories in The News, Ketchikan, Alaska. June 9, 2002.

Downey, Lynn. *"A Short History of Denim."* Levi Strauss & Company Historian 2014.

Ellsworth American, *"Sullivan News."* July 31, 1879.

Interview. *"Harry Plummer."* Sullivan, Maine. July 1994.

Kempton, C.W. *"Sketches of The New Mining District At Sullivan, Maine."* Mining Engineer, West Sullivan, Maine. March, 1880.

Maine Mining Journal. *"Milton Mine."* Published 28 West Market Square, Bangor, Maine 1880-1883.

Markey, Kevin. *"The Incredible Value of Everyday Things."* USA Weekend November 21-23, 2003.

New York Times. *"A Mining Fever in Maine."* February 4, 1879.

Philbrick, F.C. *"Economic Geology Papers."* F.C. Philbrick & Co. Stationers, 101 Devonshire, 25 Water Street, Boston. 1904.

State of Maine Legislature, Chapter 524. *"An Act to Incorporate the Long Pond Water Company."* March 6, 1885.

Stewart, William F. *"Milton Mining and Milling Co., Sullivan Silver Mining Co., Waukeag Silver Mining Co."* Geological Report 1880.

Sullivan Bulletin. *"Sullivan Region, Milton Mine."* July 8, 1880.

Underwater Archaeology Notes. *"Summer Field School 2012."* University of Maine at Machias, July 2012.

About The Authors

John Daley is a resident of Sullivan, Maine. He grew up in Sorrento, Maine, the middle child of three and received his diploma from Sumner Memorial High School, Sullivan, Maine. He attended the University of Maine at Machias, and received his B.S. Degree in Secondary Education, Major: History and Minor: Social Science. John attended the University of Maine, Orono, Maine, and received his Master's Degree in Educational Administration. He has been a public education teacher or administrator for 37 years. John became certified as an Open Water Diver through the YMCA in 1974 and in 1996 became a PADI instructor. He has since reached to level of MSDT. He has been lobster fishing for over 35 years.

Marlene Daley is a resident of Sullivan, Maine. She grew up in Chester, Maine, the youngest of 15 children and received her diploma from Mattanawcook Academy, Lincoln, Maine. She attended the University of Maine at Machias and received her A.S. Degree in Recreational Management and a B.S. Degree in Education, Major: Elementary Education. Marlene attended the University of Maine, Orono, Maine, and received her Master's Degree in Education, Major: Special Education. She has been a public education teacher or administrator for 35 years. Marlene became certified as an Open Water Diver through the YMCA in 1984 and in 1996 became a PADI instructor. She has since reached to level of MSDT.

John and Marlene (Tash) Daley were married in 1984. They have three daughters; Jessie, Tashia, and Jennie. They have been owners of the restaurant by the bridge in Sullivan since 1995. It is currently known as The Galley Restaurant.

Made in the USA
Middletown, DE
13 August 2017